GW00707301

The Complete Guide & Resource to In-Line Skating

Stephen Christopher Joyner

BETTERWAY BOOKS
Cincinnati, Ohio

Also by Stephen Christopher Joyner:
The Joy of Walking: More Than Just Exercise

Cover design by Studio 500

Typography by Blackhawk Typesetting

Prepress Services by Studio 500 Associates

Rollerblade® is a trademark of Rollerblade, Inc., and is used with their permission.

Cover photographs are courtesy of Rollerblade, Inc.

All other photographs are by Stephen C. Joyner except as noted.

Illustrations © 1993 Chris Smith.

Disclaimer:

In-line skating is an action sport that carries a significant risk of personal injury or death. Neither the author, Betterway Books, nor F & W Publications, Inc. recommends that anyone participate in this activity unless he or she is an expert, seeks qualified professional instruction or guidance, is knowledgeable of the risks associated with in-line skating, and is willing to personally assume all responsibility associated with those risks. We strongly recommend the use of quality protective equipment including wrist guards, helmet, knee and elbow pads, and gloves. Please skate safely and under control at all times.

The Complete Guide & Resource to In-Line Skating. Copyright © 1993 by Stephen Christopher Joyner. Printed and bound in the United States of America. All rights reserved. No part of this book may be reproduced in any form or by any electronic or mechanical means including information storage and retrieval systems without permission in writing from the publisher, except by a reviewer, who may quote brief passages in a review. Published by Betterway Books, an imprint of F&W Publications, Inc., 1507 Dana Avenue, Cincinnati, Ohio 45207. 1-800-289-0963. First edition.

97 96 95 94 93   5 4 3 2 1

Library of Congress Cataloging-in-Publication Data

Joyner, Stephen Christopher
    The complete guide & resource to in-line skating / Stephen Christopher Joyner.— 1st ed.
        p. cm.
    Includes bibliographical references (p.) and index.
    ISBN 1-55870-289-X : $12.95
    1. In-line skating.   I. Title. II. Title: Complete guide and resource to in-line skating.
GV859.73.J69 1993
    796.2'1 — dc20   92-37945
                                                                            CIP

For
C. Randel
With Peace and Godspeed

Acknowledgments

• •

Without the combined efforts of the following individuals, much of the material in this book — especially the In-line Skating Resource Guide — would not be possible. My sincerest thanks and appreciation to all of you.

Miriam Arie; Rick Babington; David Baum; Betterway Publications; Priscilla Boehme; Anna A. Bostedt; Harry Brennan; Jamie Budge; Ellen Bulger; Gary Chang; Tony Converse; Dave Curry; Pete Davis; Rob Davis; Brian Delaney; Jeff Dowling; Sophie Eaton; Judie Facthe; Mark Farnan; Judie Fetch; John Gill; David Gold; Rev. Michael Goldsun; Chris Hall; Bryan Hansen; Mary Haugen; Ed Hayes; Duain Hebda; Ari Horowitz; Thomas C. Howard; Joe Janasz; Chris Jones; Adlai Karim; Dean Kaese; Kari Kron; Julie G. Labach; Doug Levine; Jon Lowden; Kevin Luff; Jeff Markland; Bill Matthews; John McFadden; Tracy Mercier; Steve Merrifield; Katherine Mielke; David Miles; Brian Mirich; Milan Mitrovic; Jack Murphy; Steve Nash; Hal Newell; Rick Olson; Scott Olson; Ray Pisar; Glen Pyle; RIO II; Dan Seiden; Doug Shapiro; John Skelton; Milo Smith; Barbara Sorensen; Chartelle Tarrant; Mike Weissberger; Dian Werardi; Zachary Whittmer; Harry Wise; Shirley Yates; Tanya Zucchini; and Henry Zuver III.

And special thanks to:

Hilary Swinson. Only an author can fully appreciate the tireless efforts and exacting eye of his editor. The editor spends countless tedious hours reading, checking, amending, and deleting. My sincerest thanks and gratitude go to Hilary Swinson, my editor.

Christopher Smith. What a beautiful dimension you have given to this work. If only my words could speak as well as your images! And if only thanks was enough!

Jon Lowden of *InLine: The Skater's Magazine*. Thanks so much for all your efforts.

Kari Kron of Rollerblade® Inc. For all your great faxes, resourcefulness, and wit. Thank you.

Mike Weissberger. Thank you so much for always being there for me on a moment's notice. You are a fine friend.

Barbara Sorensen of The National Museum of Roller Skating. What would my account of the history of this great sport be without you? Greatest thanks.

Karim Adlai of Team Karim. What generosity! What superb photographs! Thank you.

Jamie Budge of WindSkate, Inc. What exhilaration you have brought to the sport! What beautiful images you have given to this book! I thank you.

Scott Olson. May the likes of you and your brothers continue to bring the world your vision and innovation.

David Miles, Ellen Bulger, Dian Weradi, Bryan Hansen, Art Brown, Jeff Dowling, Rick Babington, Mark Farnen. Thank you for your wisdom and insight.

Finally to those who responded to my hundreds of queries and sent me countless letters, brochures, catalogs, newletters, magazines, and photographs — I thank you one and all.

Foreword

No one has ever asked to me to write a foreword for a book before. It's exciting, but it's also a big responsibility.

I first spoke to Steve Joyner, the author of this book, several months ago. He telephoned me at my office and asked if I would be willing to spend some time talking to him about in-line skating. I agreed, and it wasn't long before we both were plunged into a stream-of-consciousness conversation about everything from the mixed curses and blessings of progress in all of its most terrible and promising forms, to the socially healing potential of the in-line skate. We talked about the place of emotion in our society. We talked about materialism, and its related stresses. And I finally got to go off at length about those ubiquitous stair-climbing machines we see in gyms and health clubs, yet which seem (to me, at least) to be utterly indicative of the confusion that many Americans experience regarding exercise — namely, that it has to be boring.

Steve's unusual sensitivity for thoughts and ideas not usual made me comfortable talking to him. We both agreed that in-line skates were a great idea. And we both thought cars were pretty cool, but we agreed that — like so many good ideas — the automobile is one good idea gone way, way bad.

As a society, we're increasingly isolated from the people around us, and that is mostly due to the device that begat residential sprawl — an automotive device that could cover distances easily. But at what cost? Much of the socialization that once took place on stoops, in playgrounds, or on sidewalks either doesn't happen anymore, or now takes place in the overly sanitized and controlled environs of the video arcade or shopping mall.

So much of our tax dollar is spent maintaining or patrolling roads, yet the pollution, noise, and congestion that the automobile generates take an inordinate and incalculable toll on our spirit and our physical health. In a very real sense, the automobile takes us away from our homes and keeps us from experiencing the physical world; the in-line skate, on the other hand, turns our vision in and really lets us look at where we live. Every pebble in the road, every breeze, lets us wander around inside ourselves as our hearts pound and our glands pump. We *are* animals, after all. But by disconnecting ourselves from our bodies and our environment via the automobile, we refuse to acknowledge the essential truths behind our physical needs and our physical being. This can only lead to stress.

Skaters are indebted to the contributions of the automobile. Its promise has given us the paved road, and the research and development impetus essential to the development and refinement of such complex but seemingly simple technologies as sealed roller bearings and the urethane wheel. But it *is* time for a change. Our cities — choked with motorized traffic, polluted air, and the din of internal combustion — are called home by over half the population of our country. For their sake, at least, we must change. But how? Easy. Skate — just skate. Hopefully, your quiet, clean, and healthy example will influence others to skate as well. And whatever you do, don't be afraid to tell people why you love the sport. Spread the word.

The in-line skate *is* an instrument of change. It allows us the freedom of a car or bicycle, but — unlike a car — forces us to pay for our pleasure *directly*, with sweat. That payment is an investment we should gladly make; an investment in both our health *and* our spirit.

I hope you enjoy reading this informative book as much as I have. Writing it has clearly been a labor of love for Steve Joyner. His enthusiasm and love for skating shines through very clearly, on every page. Truly, Joyner is a skate evangelist, in the truest sense of the word.

Jon Lowden
Editor, *InLine: The Skater's Magazine*

Contents

● ●

Introduction

● ●

Liberating. Exhilarating. Euphoric. Addictive. A smidgin of danger.

A new wheeled wonder has arrived that inspires rhapsody. Women, children, men — from ages four to four score — are rolling out of in-line skating stores in record numbers. Between 1986 and 1992, a once fledgling sport experienced an explosive growth rate of 6,000 percent, driving manufacturers to their production limits. Indeed, in-line skating has taken the lead as the fastest growing sport in the nation.

"In-lines," the hottest roller skates around, do not look much like the skates most baby boomers remember. The hardware of today resembles flashy ski boots with a single row of hard rubber wheels down the center of the sole. The colors are blinding. Their undulating sound hypnotic. They are known as in-line skates, but nearly everyone refers to them as Rollerblades®, based on the prototypical brand that dominates the market and has stirred a cyclone of skating hysteria.

The last twenty years have seen numerous crazes and crashes. I vaguely remember growing up and spending time around the Venice Beach boardwalk inhabited as it was with tube tops and the sounds of disco. But that was then and this is now. And in the nineties, skating has ushered

Golden Gate Park, San Francisco, Winter 1992.
Photo copyright and courtesy of Zac Wittmer.

in a new lifestyle of wheeled fun, challenge, and transportation. In-line skates are here to stay. As for the roller skate, it still has a place for now. At 130 years of age, roller skating is wheezing in popularity and just can't keep up with a sprightly young racer. But have no fear. There's plenty of road out there for them to use, as long as they stay far to the right and out of the way! Being rolled over by your offspring is a terrible way to go.

I so believe in this sport, am so convinced of the purity and joy it confers, that I shall say in earnest: *in-line skating has something to offer every one of you.* From the champion in-line speed skater to the dubious novice, skating is fun, readily accessible, and easy to learn, but most of all, it is here for everyone. GET IN-LINE!

1.
The Origins of In-Line Skating

●●●

Zzzzmmmmm, Whhhishhhhh. Look around. Everywhere you cast your eyes, you are bound to see relentless, flowing movement. Cars, baby strollers, wheelchairs are everywhere. Garbage trucks, Tonka™ trucks, and hand trucks. Earth movers, conveyor belts, and elevators. There seems to be no end to it all. From long ago, the boundless human imagination has continued to tinker with his ancestors' inventions. From sticks and stones to arrows and daggers, time and innovation march on, rendering the "latest and greatest" obsolete. Man, wholly determined, rages onward, of single mind and purpose to "reinvent" the wheel.

THE WHEEL

The invention of the wheel is among the greatest milestones of all time. Remarkably, however, such gargantuan wonders as the Sphinx and the Egyptian pyramids were constructed without the utility of the wheel.

The precise date and place of the wheel's discovery remain inconclusive, although many experts believe that it was invented just once and then broadly diffused throughout the world. With this knowledge, other civilizations utilized and improved upon the wheel's basic design. Of course, the Greeks and Romans were the first to use the wheel extensively. With their system of roads, bridges, and horse-drawn carts, these civilizations made giant advances in construction, commerce, and the military, all due in large part to this fantastic, cornerless device. Thus, having been so lauded by these powerful civilizations, the wheel — and all its derivative uses — was poised to serve all humanity.

SKATING ON ICE: EARLY YEARS AND THE MIDDLE AGES

Quick and independent locomotion has preoccupied the mind of man from time immemorial. Despite his determination to ease the work of personal movement, however, winter's harsh chill always coated the ground with ice. So if the ice could not be moved, then man would make use of it. And from this premise, the first "scate" was made.[1]

Despite the existence of several theories, man probably first skated on ice using sharp splinters of animal bone fitted to the bottom of boots. Artifacts discovered in Holland, Sweden, Iceland, and England indicate that skating over ice was prevalent at least from 11 A.D. Actual evidence of their use is found in drawings, along with references in literature to ice skating, dating from the Middle Ages (circa 1000 to 1400 A.D.).

THE BIRTH OF A SPORT

Ice skating as a recreational sport developed on the lakes of Scotland and the canals of the Netherlands in the thirteenth and fourteenth centuries. About this time, wood was substituted for bone in skate blades. In 1572, the first iron skates were manufactured. Not only did the iron blades reduce the friction between skate and ice, but their resistance to lateral slippage enabled skaters to advance themselves. In time, skating manuals were published, and the first skate club was founded in Edinburgh in 1742. Thanks to Scottish immigrants, metal-bladed skates soon made their way across the Atlantic and were introduced in North America.

Ice skating did not develop as an organized, competitive sport until the introduction of steel skate blades, which could be permanently attached to leather boots. The earliest iron blades dulled and rusted quickly, and the shoes to which they were strapped lacked support and insulation. Using steel skates, however, U.S. ballet dancer Jackson Haines created a free-flowing skating technique that incorporated waltz-like movements. Ice speed skating, which had developed in the Netherlands in the seventeenth century, was given a boost by the innovations in skate construction. Figure skating became an Olympic event in 1908. In the 1924 Olympic Games, men's speed skating became an official event.

So there it is — the birth of the skate and of the wheel. Unfortunately, the inventor of the first roller skate is not known. Historians suggest that it was in Holland, where one particular skating fiend could not bear the spring and summer off his skates, so an off-season skate was developed. This individual produced a wheeled skate with several wooden spools in a line. Ironically, some 200 years later, a similar frustration would entice a couple of high school students to reinvent the in-line skate so that they could play ice hockey year round.

A CLUMSY GENIUS

He should have been called the Wizard. Joseph Merlin, the first person *recorded* as the inventor of the roller skate, is remembered as a brilliant craftsman who brought humor and a dash of magic to the birth of the roller skate. A deft designer of musical instruments and a nifty mechanic, Merlin was held in considerable esteem for his work, and was invited to the Royal Academy of Science in 1760. Soon he took on the directorship of the Cox Museum, where he showcased an array of his musical creations — a violin and a piano, to name a few. He exhibited many of his other designs throughout London, one of which was a pair of roller skates.

Next, on a now infamous evening, Merlin attended a masquerade party in Soho Square. Donning a clumsy costume while playing the violin, Merlin began moving about the room with his wheeled contraptions strapped to his feet. He soon realized, however, that he could not turn or brake. With the folly of a circus act, he slammed through a huge and expensive mirror, smashing it to bits, wounding himself, smashing his violin, and, alas, sending the roller skate into hibernation for thirty years.[2]

ROLLING ONWARD

In 1790, the roller skate, or "ground skate" as it was dubbed, made a popular, albeit brief, appearance in Paris and parts of Germany. It was not until 1818 that roller skates "made" the ballet entitled "The Artist, or Winter Pleasures" in Berlin. It was impossible at the time to make ice for a stage production, so roller skates were used instead. And as time would prove, roller skates would make further "stage appearances."

The following year, yet another designer, Monsieur Petibled, designed a roller skate and touted it as a dry land equivalent to the ice skate. However, his high expectations for the skate were dashed, as turning a corner required an unreasonable amount of physical exertion.[3]

THE FIRST GLIMPSE OF IN-LINE SKATES

According to historical records, every early roller skate designer utilized a four-wheel chassis (a pair of wheels under each end of the boot). Not until 1823 did Robert John Tylers break the mold. His "Volito" skate, employed for the first time, used five wheels in a single line. Also unprecedented was the ability to turn left or right by using larger center wheels (based on "rockering" wheels of today). Augmenting the design's practicality, Tylers fashioned hooks in the front and back of the Volito as a braking system. Unfortunately, despite superior technical design, the skate's popularity just did not catch on.[4]

Without a following and/or broad exposure, efforts to perfect a popular "user-friendly" roller skate seemed futile. Still, it survived and made another stage appearance, also in 1823. Roller skates were "cast" by the ballet master, Robillon, in "The Alpine Dairy Maid." To simulate some of the winter scenes, the performers wore wheeled skates to represent ice skates.

The designing of skates continued. Some looked liked tricycles, some set wheels high, and others low. Although the designer "wheeled shoes" continued to be well-received on stage, they hardly got a nod anywhere else.[5]

For the next two decades, roller skating continued to go unnoticed. During the 1830s, roller skates were used occasionally for stage productions and some outdoor exhibitions, but nothing widespread. Although no gimmicks or "hooks" were used to attract attention, a galvanizing effort was needed.

The Germans knew just what was required. Pretty women and beer! In the late 1840s, roller skates were hitched up with these two in a beer tavern known as the Corso Halle in Berlin. Thirsty patrons were served by three or four young waitresses on wheels. A newspaper of the day explains it best:

The moment a new customer takes his seat, one of the damsels darts from the end of the room, skims over the floor, describes clever curves round the end of a table, or a cluster of chairs, brings herself up at the moment he thinks it inevitable she must glide over his toes, and requests to know his wishes ... She often collects several orders in the course of a round or from a single group; and will skate back with any number of glass pint pots of beer in both hands, without disturbing a flake of froth. Except from the rattling noise produced, the motion is as good an imitation of [ice] skating as can be conceived. To the curious stranger, no secret is made of the mechanisms employed: Small iron wheels, let into the sole of a strong, but neatly fitting pair of boots, are all the mystery; but to move about in them easily, and even gracefully, requires much practice. It is also more fatiguing than walking; and towards midnight, when it may be assumed that each waitress has skated several miles, they look rather weary.[6]

Popularity thus achieved, roller skating was poised for its greatest accolades in the Grand Opera. Not once, but twice, during 1849 roller skating was accorded the great honor of playing a paramount role in successful stage presentations; at once earning more public interest, admiration, and enthusiasm than it had in all the years before with its accidents, exhibitions, and inventions.

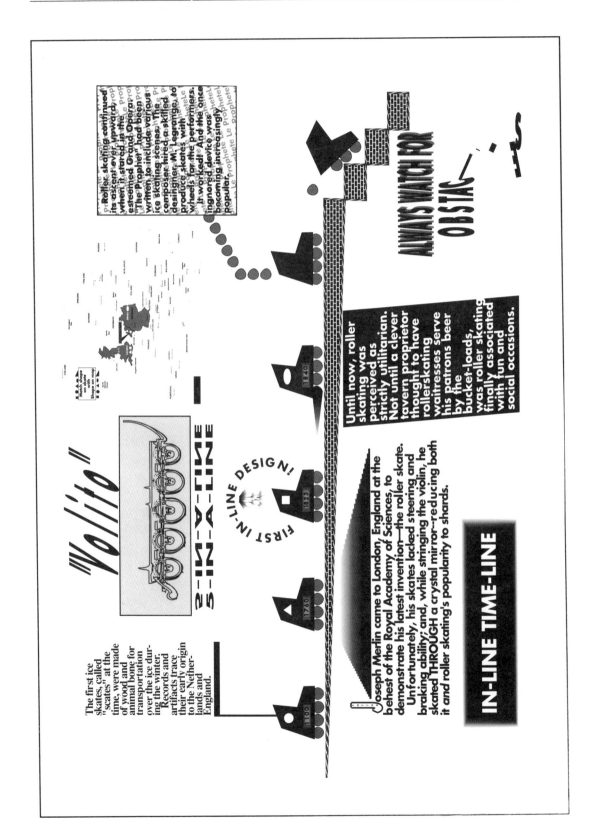

IN-LINE TIME-LINE

The first ice skates, called "scates," at the time, were made of wood and animal bone for transportation over the ice during the winter. Records and artifacts trace their early origin to the Netherlands and England.

Joseph Merlin came to London, England at the behest of the Royal Academy of Sciences, to demonstrate his latest invention—the roller skate. Unfortunately, his skates lacked steering and braking ability; and, while stringing the violin, he skated THROUGH a crystal mirror--reducing both it and roller skating's popularity to shards.

Until now, roller skating was perceived as strictly utilitarian. Not until a clever tavern proprietor thought to have rollerskating waitresses serve his patrons beer by the bucket-loads, was roller skating finally associated with fun and social occasions.

Roller skating continued its ascent ever upward, when it stared in the esteemed Grand Opera "The Prophet," had been written to include various ice skating scenes. The composer hired a skilled designer, M. Legrange, to produce skates with wheels for the performers. It worked! And the once ignored device was becoming increasingly popular.

"Volito"

2-IN-A-LINE
5-IN-A-LINE

FIRST IN-LINE DESIGN!

ALWAYS WATCH FOR OBSTACLES

Match shape on skate with Shape on map

Rollerblade, Inc. World Headquarters

MINNESOTA
Duluth
Minneapolis
St. Paul

1981 ®

U
S
A
C • R
C

The Skating of Independently-operated roller

The United States Amateur Confederation (1867) Roller part of Independently-operated roller sports, formally based on its Detroit, 1867, the Skating (USAC/RS) Skating incorporated in as a portion and recognized all competition, as the hitherto roller in present Association, 1973 - RS is Body-Roller. Originally / to -. USAC/RS is Body-roller. Originally / to Governing United States- released in 1968. the Confederation in Confederation Needed location of

Central Park
New York City

The Plimpton skate was a vast improvement over previous skate designs. The wheels could curve inwards, allowing tight turns. The wheels were made of box wood and fitted with loose ball bearings, increasing their performance. The skate was attached to the shoe with leather straps. Available in sizes from 7 1/2 to 11 1/2, the PLYMPTON SKATE sold for $3.00.

Circular Roller Skating

ROLLER SKATES' STAGE DEBUT

Meyerbeer (1791-1864), the lauded German composer, had written his opera *The Prophet*.[7] No one had invented a successful method of producing synthetic ice, or of transferring the natural variety indoors and keeping it fit to skate upon. It thus became necessary to devise a skate for use on a wooden surface. Meyerbeer consulted M. Legrange, a machinist. Whether Legrange knew anything of the previous models of roller skates is not known. At any rate, he produced a crude skate running on iron wheels. The skate worn by the many members of the cast had two wheels in a straight line, placed some distance from each other. The female performers in the ballet were provided four-wheeled skates, not in a straight line but coupled, placing less side-to-side stress on their knees.

At about the same time, Paul Taglioni, a ballet composer and choreographer, wrote and devised "Les Plaisirs de l'Hiver ou, Les Patineurs" ("The Pleasures of Winter or, The Skaters"). Set in a winter sports scene, roller skates were used to resemble the blade of an ice skate. The stage was covered with a sheet of smooth material to represent the frozen river. The music was composed to help describe the sports of a Hungarian winter, "even imitating the sound of gliding on ice," as a critic who reviewed the ballet described it. The scenery, costumes, dancing, and music drew large crowds and great praise, but the achievement of the performers on wheeled skates created a sensation unrivaled in the day.

The continuous applause and cheers had a tremendous effect in giving roller skating the stimulus that it so badly needed. In 1857, rinks were opened to the public in Floral Hall at Covent Garden and in the Strand, London. The skates used at these rinks had four iron wheels extending in a straight line from the toe to the heel. The friction was enormous because of the crude manner in which the skates were constructed. Therefore, "edges" (i.e., curves) were extremely difficult to execute.

It was on skates of this type that Jackson Haines later gave his roller exhibitions. Haines, an American ballet master, took up and mastered ice skating and he brought forth new ideas, freedom, and rhythm in skating. In 1864, he created a sensation in Europe with his figure skating. His free and graceful style was adopted throughout the world and later became known as the International Style. During the years 1864 and 1865, he presented exhibitions in the Alhambra, London, and in the skating ballet of "Le Prophéte" in several European cities.[8]

In 1852, Joseph Gidman patented a skate with a coupled wheel in the middle and single wheels at each end. The Woodward skate was fitted with rollers made of vulcanized India rubber, those in the middle being slightly larger than the ones at each end — somewhat like the skates originated by Tylers — thus making it slightly easier to accomplish turns. The rubber wheels were also superior to the iron ones previously used because they clung to wooden boards without any tendency to slip sideways. An American named Shaler also introduced a skate with rubber rollers, which he advertised and sold as the "Parlour Skate."

Other skates were soon introduced in rapid succession. A skate with four pairs of coupled wheels, which could be placed at some distance apart for beginners or closer together for more experienced skaters, was introduced. This was followed by one aptly called the "Wheelbarrow" skate; it had a large pair of rear wheels and a smaller wheel in the front. However, none of these skates could be guided in "edges," or curves, except at the expense of tremendous friction and exertion. Most, if not all, of the figures that made ice skating a popular pastime were impossible to accomplish with wheeled skates on a wooden floor.

THE BIRTH OF THE MODERN ROLLER SKATE

Although the year 1863 has gone down in the annals of history as the year Abraham Lincoln spun the wheels of freedom by signing the Emancipation Proclamation, the wheels of roller skating made strides forward of a different sort. With the development of a "circular running skate," Americans were smitten with the freedom to roll in any direction they pleased. Thanks to the foresight and determination of James L. Plimpton, the joys of roller skating endure for posterity.[9]

Having improved his health by an invigorating season of ice skating in Central Park, Plimpton longed for such exercise year round. Convinced that "artificial" ice was a failure for indoor skating, and knowing that no roller skate had ever been perfected, especially in the area of turning, James Plimpton was determined to effect change.

A furniture maker and inventor by trade, Plimpton conceived of a skating design principle which is still used today. His invention, called the "circular running skate," gave the skater the latitude to execute the graceful skating arc which since has evolved as skating's striking visual mark. Plimpton's genius allowed him to develop and employ a rubber cushioning device in his roller skate; thus enabling the skater to make smooth turns by shifting his weight — a vast improvement over earlier designs that required sheer force to turn.[10]

Plimpton did not rest with his invention. He pushed skating to its logical apex, opening the first roller skating rink, forming a skating club, and promoting the first "roller competitions." Still, for all of Plimpton's contributions, skating did not become a public attraction. He worked diligently to bring roller skating to the "educated and refined" classes across the country. Civic officials, clergy, the press, professionals, and other high society members flocked to roll in Plimpton's rinks. Roller skating eventually opened its door to the masses, and with this came the need for organization.

USAC/RS AND THE '70s

In 1937, the United States Amateur Confederation of Roller Skating (USAC/RS) was founded as part of the Roller Skating Rink Operators Association (RSROA). In 1973, USAC/RS independently incorporated, thus becoming the official governing body for all roller sports in the country. Today, USAC/RS has 23,000-plus members and more than 1,600 skating clubs across the country. In addition, USAC/RS plays an active role in fielding TEAM USA for the Pan American games and the Olympics in three skating disciplines: speed, artistic, and roller hockey.[11]

After USAC/RS's incorporation in 1973, roller skating's popularity increased. Soon the Venice Beach boardwalk, characterized by tube tops, tacky colors, and disco music, became roller skaters' haven for every walk of life and persuasion. Roller skating reached its zenith in the late '70s, as interest in the skateboard was renewed. In 1979, Golden Gate Park was deluged with some 20,000 roller skaters on weekends. Such large numbers wreaked havoc on surrounding communities and neighborhoods, as homeowners' gardens were rolled over, garages were used as urinals, and pedestrians found walking hazardous to their health. This mess and the resulting backlash was tagged by the media as the Great Skate Debate of San Francisco.[12] After months of wrangling with community officials, a portion of the park was set aside for the exclusive use of the skating community. Today, with minds put at ease with the help of the Golden Gate Skate Patrol (equipped with radios and trained in CPR), the Park cordons off an area for skaters to use free of traffic, every Sunday from dawn to dusk. Today in San Francisco, all is well on the skating front.

THE '80S: ROLLERBLADE® PUTS AMERICA IN MOTION

In 1979, Scott Olson, a nineteen-year-old Minneapolis native and semi-pro hockey player, was browsing in a sporting goods store when he came across a pair of in-line skates.

In-lines, as you may recall, originated in the Netherlands in the 1700s, so Olson cannot claim to have conceived of the basic design. He did, however, fashion an in-line skate for off-season hockey, as he was frustrated that his standard off-season training routine was lacking. His teammates agreed, and soon he was building skates in his basement and hawking them door to door.

By 1981, he had quit playing hockey and launched a company. In 1984, a lot of skate peddling later, he was pressed to sell most of his holdings to Minneapolis investor Robert O. Naegele, Jr., the current chairman of Rollerblade®. Today, Olson has no share in the company he founded, a company estimated to sell $200 million of in-line skates and equipment in 1993.

Following the buyout, Rollerblade® launched an aggressive marketing campaign. Rollerblade® has proven a savvy marketer on its own. To cultivate its on-the-edge image, Rollerblade® has largely skirted Madison Avenue. Instead, the company has taken its own advice and hit the road. Its Rock 'N' Rollerblade Tour features twenty-five skaters in black and neon outfits, touring America performing stunts and skate dancing at campuses, playgrounds, and theme parks.

In one way, Rollerblade® may be becoming too successful. Its name is practically synonymous with in-line skating, and that puts Rollerblade® in potential jeopardy of losing its trademark, as aspirin and cellophane did. So the company is shifting its marketing focus from promoting in-line skating to shaping a distinctive brand image. Rollerblade® has hired advertising agencies and is preparing its first national TV campaign. In selected sporting goods stores around the country, exclusive Rollerblade® boutiques are being test marketed.

Despite its successes, Rollerblade® has kept rolling its innovative wheels. The company currently has over 185 patents, many of which have not been introduced to the public. One of its most recent concepts is the MetroBlade™, an in-line skate that easily converts into a pair of shoes for those skate-to/walk-in occasions and, according to a top official at Rollerblade®, the company has a hand-held, cable activated braking system nearly ready for market. It is further responsible for the use of polyurethane boots and wheels, metal frames, dual bearings, heel brakes, and the first non-metal frame and wheel with a core, both of which add speed and comfort while skating.

Meanwhile, as sales double and triple annually, competing manufacturers are eager to snatch away some of Rollerblade®'s seventy percent market share.[13] First Team Sports Inc., number two in in-line skate sales, is coming on strong with Wayne Gretzky promoting its Ultra-Wheels line. Canstar Sports follows in the in-line fray with its Bauer® brand skate. (Incidentally, First Team Sports Inc. and Canstar Sports are currently the only publicly traded companies in the industry.) Other competitors include CCM Maska, California Pro USA, NüSkate, and dozens of component part manufacturers. With Rollerblade®'s most popular skates retailing for $139 and $199, Taiwanese knockoffs, some priced below $50, are grabbing share at the low end. Even Fisher-Price® has jumped in, with kids' skates that can be adjusted for growing feet.

Team Rollerblade®/Kryptonics was founded in 1989 and is currently managed by Tom Schuler of Team Sports International, Waukesha, WI. Former team members include Eddy Matzger, current holder of the one-hour world record and considered to be among the best all-around in-line skaters in the country. Current team members include Eric Flaim, U.S. Olympic

The in-line skate. This one is manufactured by Rollerblade®, Inc.

Scott B. Olson, inventor and developer of both the original Rollerblade® skate and the SwitchIt Interchangeable Skate System. Courtesy of Scott B. Olson.

silver medalist at Calgary and winner of the IISA 10K 1991 Nationals at Irvine, CA; and Karen Edwards, who has won more competitions than any other woman to date.[14]

THE SECOND MILLENIUM AND BEYOND

As the in-line market begins to mature, expect to see more ways to skate in-line introduced. In-line roller hockey, also known as street hockey, is already making its mark as it is the only in-line activity that offers the camaraderie and competition that is the mainstay of team sports. Also coming into vogue is in-line aerobics — combining the best of aerobics, in-line skating, and up-tempo music. And believe it or not, Scott Olson, present owner of O.S. Designs and NüSkate, has introduced in-line tennis. According to Olson, who contends that he is more an inventor than anything else, it's a lot of fun. When asked if he thinks in-line tennis will convert a nation of devout players to don in-lines in lieu of tennis shoes, he says, "Who cares? It's fun."

PROFILE: SCOTT OLSON

Author: Why did you build a skate in the first place?

Scott Olson: I used to dream about being able to ice skate to school for transportation, like down the alley and stuff. When I got my first pair of in-lines, it was a dream come true. I could skate in the summertime.

A: So you don't claim to have invented in-line skates?

O: Right. There have been a lot of people who have invented skates and for one reason or another, it never worked out.

A: How did the first Rollerblade® skate evolve? What is its history?

O: I got involved with what was to become Rollerblade® in about 1979. I was just out of high school and my brother and I happened to buy a pair of skates down at the local sporting goods shop. I tried them out, liked them, and went back to see if he would sell me some more skates. I took the rest of his inventory. Later, I came back to see if he would sell me any more. Well, this guy wanted nothing to do with me, so I ended selling these skates directly for the manufacturer, Super Sport Skate Company in California.

Ultimately, I brought on other employees, my brother Brennan being the first, then Jim, Chuck, Todd, and Luke to sell the Super Street Skate. I couldn't get any retailer to carry it, so I established my own sales network selling directly to the consumer all over the country.

A: So the Super Street Skate was the precursor to the first Rollerblade® skate?

O: Yes. I made improvements in the wheel with a double bearing wheel design, and bought a skate patent from the Chicago Skate Company to make further refinements in the wheel and frame assembly.

A: Where did the Rollerblade® name come from?

O: There are a lot of people out there who take credit for the trademarked name and the logo. Actually, there is just one guy who came up with the logo. A friend of mine was writing a business plan for my company as a class assignment. That's when we came up with the logo that you see today. As for the name, well, that kind of evolved. We started calling it the Ultimate

Street Skate, but it was really the consumers who coined the term Rollerblade®. And I later signed the trademark to make it official.

A: Are you concerned that the sport may be hurt by a lot of inexpensive and cheaply made in-line skates from Asian manufacturers?

O: Well, as long as you get a molded plastic shell that gives you the support that you have to have, and good quality bearings and wheels, I don't think there is that much junk out there yet. But you get what you pay for.

A: Do you see major shoe manufacturers like Nike® or Reebok® buying into the industry and taking over Rollerblade® or one of the smaller companies?

O: My prediction is that these shoe companies are going to get involved, and they are going to change a lot about how these skates look. It's going to become part of the shoe market with more emphasis on fit and comfort than before.

You know the Lightning boot was the first boot I brought in from Italy, and it is a hockey boot. And it never went over for hockey, so we marketed it as a recreational ice skate. It went over well because it gave people the support they needed, but it was an over-built boot to begin with. Even women were skating with it, and it wasn't even designed for a woman's foot.

A: I have heard several industry opinion leaders say they anticipate retail sales reaching a billion dollars by 1995. Would you agree with that? And how about the number of in-line skaters by 1995 as well?

O: Oh, sure. I like to deal in wholesale dollars and I am predicting a half billion in wholesale dollars by 1995. As far as participants, based on an average skate cost of $100, I would predict between 40 and 50 million skaters by '95.

A: Do you find yourself more of an inventor at heart, or an in-line skate entrepreneur?

O: Well, my goal is to stay ahead of the game in product innovation.

A: Let me try again. If in-line skating didn't exist and you saw that a kitchen blender could be improved, would you improve it? Are you an "innate" inventor, or something else?

O: There are a lot of things I have invented. And that's my challenge — to see if I can pull it off with another product line. That's why I want to get Nüskate going, because it is a place where I can introduce my products. Inventing something is half the battle. Selling it is the other half.

A: To what do you attribute the astronomical growth of the in-line skate industry?

O: I think that word of mouth would have worked in time. But certainly Bob Naegele, who put the money in the company to get the word out, should be patted on the back. You know the product was there and it was dynamite, but money is king.

A: What do you think of Rollerblade®'s highly praised marketing campaign?

O: Well, it has basically been grass roots marketing. You know, hitting the road in vans and showing the public the products. It is something that I did from the very beginning. I was convinced that everyone who tried them would be sold instantly. The dealers and the public loved those clinics we did. And we loved it because it made sales. And of course the media loved it. People like yourself saw what was happening, and wanted to do a story on it — and that was free.

You know I have always said the product makes you do things you normally wouldn't do.

A: Some say the same thing about money.

O: (Laughs.) Yeah, that's true. But look. Old men are doing it. Or people like Bob Naegele who never thought they would put this kind of money into a deal like this. All kinds of stories. I knew that the product would do what it has done. It was just too good. You know, it's changed people's lives, and it has attracted a good group of professional business people to get involved in it. It's dynamite!

A: When you're not obsessing about skates, what else do you enjoy doing? Do you skate?

O: Oh yeah. I also work a lot. I play night golf with a glow ball. I love that. And in September is my first ever Roller Tennis tournament. I have been playing for six years.

A: Roller Tennis?

O: Yeah, I'm working on promoting this. Stay tuned.

A: Can you share your opinions on the governing bodies of this sport: USAC/RS and IISA?

O: Well, as far as USAC/RS, I don't think they have done anything for the in-line sport. I mean, they were really against in-line skates in the beginning. But if they don't get on the bandwagon with in-line skates, they're going to be sitting there holding onto nothing because nobody's going to be skating on conventional roller skates in five years. Those things are going to be obsolete. That's my prediction.

A: Skating safely has received a lot of attention in this sport with the likes of the SKATESMART campaign. Is the freedom to choose to wear or not to wear safety equipment more important, or is protecting the uninitiated skater from his or her own lack of experience and ability more important? Where does the responsibility of skating safely begin and where does it end?

O: That's a very good question. Freedom of choice, you know, is always an argument. I'd be inclined to go with it, but when you mention the people who are naive and beginners, I think we have a responsibility to get them to at least consider wearing safety equipment.

2.
Benefits of In-Line Skating

In-line skating is one of the few sport activities that contributes to both anaerobic (muscle-building) and aerobic (cardiovascular) fitness. Although both anaerobic and aerobic fitness are vital to a full and healthy life, most fitness mavens focus primarily on their aerobic health. With the widespread attention on heart disease, potential heart disease sufferers have been encouraged by the media, their doctors, and perhaps the ill health of their friends and family to "aerobicize" — run, swim, use treadmills — anything to keep their heart rate increased for at least twenty minutes.

Unfortunately, anaerobic fitness, the other half of physical fitness, has received relatively scant attention. Bone disease, atrophy of the skeleton and bones, and susceptibility to illness and injury can be greatly reduced by a lifetime of mild anaerobic exercise. Any activity that builds strength, as opposed to the endurance that aerobic exercise yields, is referred to as anaerobic.

For the millions who have become addicted to in-line skating, the list of words that have come to be used to refer to their experience is long and flattering to the sport. Rarely, however, will one find both anaerobic and aerobic used in one breath. Unlike exercise or fitness sports that people use solely to improve their health, in-line skating offers the thrill and sense of freedom rarely experienced while running, swimming, lifting weights, or working out in a health club. Because the in-liner is not restricted to an exercise bench or athletic club, the sensory experiences of the in-line skater are limited only by his course.

LOW IMPACT

One of the first things you will realize once you have skated a bit is how little stress or impact skating places on your bones and joints. Unlike the high-impact sports such as running, skating places less impact on the musculoskeletal system, which limits the risk of pounding away at the fragile joints of the ankle and knee.

GOOD EXERCISE

The natural conditions of our present life no longer give us enough physical activity. Work and travel are increasingly sedentary, and leisure often is a matter of watching something. (It has been estimated that people spend an average seventy-five hours spectating — films, television, sports — for every hour spent in physical participation.) So we have to plan and work to achieve enough activity to keep us physically fit.

Super-fit on in-lines. Ken Moody, in-line skating instructor.
Courtesy of Crunch, New York City.

One morning at my favorite coffee dive in San Francisco, I saw a woman wearing in-line skates. I thought I would introduce myself and ask her a few questions. I believe that her response to my last question encapsulates in the simplest terms what is so special about in-lining for your health. I asked her, "So, what did you buy your skates for? Fitness, weekend recreation, racing, cross-training?" She smiled and replied, "Fun fitness."

JUST IN TIME FOR THE 1990S

Best estimates indicate that upwards of ten million in-line skaters are rolling within, up, over, and through the air of the U.S. After talking with hundreds of skaters, only one related in-line skating to the state of our bustling planet. He duly noted that the planet is continuously rolled over with asphalt and poured with pavement. And who but the in-line skater so savors a fresh blacktop, wheezing in the asphyxiating fumes though delighting in the asphalt's virgin finish.

What of the ease in maintaining, securing, and transporting your skates? Just for argument's sake, consider the cost of tuning your bicycle, securing it from thieving hands, or checking it at the airline counter, destined to be chucked and buried under a heap of luggage.[15]

SOCIAL BENEFITS

Aside from walking, I know of no other cardiovascular sport as conducive to talking with another person as in-line skating is. Even at a fairly brisk pace, you and your skating partner will not be so utterly out of breath that you cannot converse at all.

When in-line skates first appeared on the scene with roller skates and skateboards, they seemed at once susceptible to the "skate and destroy," pseudo-rebellious culture of the late 1970s and much of the 1980s. But thanks to the countless efforts of pro-skating advocates throughout cities big and small, in-line skating not only avoided that stigma but triumphed in capturing widespread appeal. With an average age of about twenty-seven and a fifty-fifty man-to-woman split, in-line skating reflects the diverse society at large.

PRACTICAL TRANSPORTATION

Jon Lowden, Editor of *InLine: The Skater's Magazine*, does not own a car. He skates or bikes from home to work every day, a distance of about six miles. And lest he miss driving, Jon gets stopped for being a "pedestrian in the roadway" — currently eight warnings and counting. "It's for your own safety," he is reminded each time. "Close the road," Jon mutters under his breath. What better way could there be to get to your job each day, free of traffic and honking cars? By skating to work, you can avoid confined space, sitting idle, searing holes in the ozone, and wasting time.

Ask yourself, indeed challenge yourself, to a healthful, invigorating, and head-turning commute. But, for your own sake, please wear a helmet. And before you ask how you will carry a briefcase, business clothes, and toiletries while skating, refer to the In-line Skating Resource Guide under Enrge Sports and Rollerguard™. Both manufacture some great utilitarian devices that will put your questions to rest.

ACCESSIBILITY

The world is large and complicated. Our government (aka "the system") — enveloped as it is in policy, procedure, and forms in duplicate, triplicate, and so on — makes the simplicity of in-line skating refreshing. Stop. Lace on your skates. Go.

In-line and taking the lead.

What other sport or activity, excluding perhaps walking, is so immediately available as in-line skating? Think a moment. At a minimum (excluding the absurdly wealthy), in order to play a game of tennis, you need to find a court on which to play, usually wait until it is available, and often pay a rental fee as well. Golf is worse. Team sports and one-on-one activities require planning and confirmation, to say nothing of someone canceling and ruining your plans.

Consider all this further and it disputes the fairly common perception that in-line skating is financially inaccessible. Most recreational or lifestyle sports are laden with equipment. Although tennis balls may set you back a mere five dollars, consider the cost of a racket, court fees, finding a compatible partner, fuel to get there, and perhaps even a speeding ticket when you are running late!

3.
General Health

● ●

Despite the onslaught of diseases, studies show that human beings and the daily lifestyle decisions they make have the most profound effect on their overall wellness and longevity. Although annual coronary deaths have decreased by about a third since the late 1960s, this is due in large measure to the enormous advances made in medicine and heart surgery techniques. Nevertheless, no surgeon on earth can remove the years of neglect and abuse to which the average American subjects himself.

SMOKING (A COMMENTARY)

Every smoker knows the feeling. You have given up; you tell the world you have given up; the world thinks you have given up. Then you excuse yourself and snatch a fevered puff. You think the world does not notice, but it always does.

Despite the thousands of medical, governmental, and individual studies conducted, citing the ultimate doom and gloom of cigarette smoking, millions continue to asphyxiate themselves with smoking's noxious cloud. Smoking accounts for more than twenty percent of all deaths from heart disease, which in and of itself is the number one killer, and more than doubles a person's chance of dying at any given age.

Many think, albeit incorrectly, that they are relatively safe from heart disease or lung cancer because they are "light" smokers or they use only low-tar, low-nicotine brands. Yet those who smoke only one cigarette a day increase their risk of coronary death by upwards of seventy percent.

What is peculiar and ironic to me and many non-smokers is to see smokers, especially our friends, dedicate themselves to five a.m. wake-up calls to go to the gym in the name of health. What I notice, however, is that very few smokers participate in any aerobic activity. Their soot-coated lungs, gasping for air, are not capable of generating enough oxygen to fuel their bodies.

Thus afflicted, smokers regularly experience shortness of breath and/or a chronic cough. A smoker's oxygen transport ability is tremendously reduced, due to the smoke's carbon dioxide replacing the blood's oxygen.

There is some light amid all this darkness. It is never too late to stop. Kicking the habit, even after decades of smoking, is the first step you can take toward increasing your longevity. In fact, it is estimated that the likelihood of heart failure is cut in half after being smoke-free for just one year. While gliding purposefully on your skates will not stop you from smoking, the euphoria and joy that impels you to get in-line can be harnessed to slow this destructive, and often deadly, habit.

WEIGHT

The American stigma of overweight is troubling. The overweight encounter excessive teasing, ridicule, prejudice, and rejection. Thus embattled, they are apt to turn inward, denigrating

Mike Riddle, Anna Stubbs, and Greg LeVien.
Copyright 1992 and courtesy of Team Karim.

themselves due to low self-esteem. They may encounter psychological problems such as poor body image, a sense of failure, a passive/defeatist approach to life situations, and an unrealistic fear of rejection. It is naive to think that this problem begins or ends based on where a needle lands on a scale.

What Can Be Done about Excess Body Fat?

For your weight to remain constant, you must use up as many calories as you take in. When the amounts are not balanced, your weight changes. There are approximately 3,500 calories in one pound of stored body fat. For instance, if you take in an extra 500 calories a day, you will gain about one pound of body fat every seven days (500 x 7 = 3,500). Fortunately, the reverse is also true. If you take in 500 calories *less* a day than you need, you will lose about one pound every seven days. The healthiest and most effective way to lose body fat is to maintain a well-balanced diet *along with* regular, moderate exercise.

Exercise burns calories. When you use your muscles, they require energy. The more often your muscles contract, the more calories your body consumes. Indeed, doctors concur that exercise is the key to increasing lean body weight — turning fat into muscle. The failure rate of many diet plans is high because exercise is not included in weight management programs.

A Blight on Humanity

Anyone who suffers from a disease, and this I know from experience, often feels scared and vulnerable. If you have a weight problem, and uncontrollable weight *is* a disease, you are vulnerable as well. Although this is not headline news, there are more than a few diet plans run by two-bit charlatans with the scruples of repeat felons, who will tell you what you want to hear, help you lose weight fast, but leave you on your own in keeping it off. The truth is that anyone might lose weight through diuretics, steam, perspiration enhancement, body wraps, extracts, and other gimmicks, but only you and a proven system will enable you to lose weight and *keep it off*.

A Word on Spot Reduction

It is a common misconception that you can lose weight from a specific area of your body by working that specific body area. Many people err in thinking that by doing countless sit-ups, they will remove fat from the abdominal area. Regrettably, spot reduction does not work. Localized exercises, however, will help to build up muscle underneath the body fat, and in doing so will actually shrink the tissue underneath the fat, as muscle tissue is more condensed than fat tissue.

MANAGING STRESS

Your ability to manage stress affects your mental and physical health. Too much stress can lead to high blood pressure, heart disease, depression, schizophrenia, indigestion, an increased cholesterol level, stilted concentration, low back pain, headaches, cancer, and a lower resistance to pain. Too little stress is also harmful. It may contribute to boredom, loneliness, depression, and possibly, suicidal tendencies.

We adapt best to stress in the middle of the extremes. Positive stress enhances our ability to perform by helping us to overcome laziness and motivating us to be productive and excel. As with many things in life, moderation is best. Ideally, one's level of stress should be somewhere between having too much to do and being completely bored.

Looking cool, but taking chances by not wearing protective gear.

A healthy strategy for dealing with too much stress is regular exercise. In-lining helps to release muscular tension by rhythmically contracting your muscles. Like most sustained aerobic activities, skating leaves a lingering sensation of calm and vitality.

Sustained aerobic skating simulates a mini-vacation and a respite from the pressures of your daily routine. It provides a time to be by yourself or with others, depending on what best suits you. I know of many who swear by skating. Their relationships are healthier, their once-burdensome expectations of others are let go, and financial difficulties are put into perspective. Any aerobic exercise is emotionally superior to the stop-and-go sports of golf or tennis (and superior still to a bruising, disfiguring physical contact sport), yet I find that no sport reduces stress-related tension as effectively and as efficiently as lone rhythmic strides on the open road.

4.
Fitness

● ●

CALORIES BURNED — RUNNING VERSUS IN-LINE SKATING

Despite the potential damage running can incur on your musculoskeletal system, few activities equal or exceed running with regard to calories burned and improved heart rate. Notwithstanding this fact, in-line skating will take you closer to *overall* fitness than running ever will. Recreational in-liners burn roughly 280-290 calories in a thirty-minute workout. Because skaters can exercise longer and with less fatigue than runners, their *overall* caloric consumption is often greater than that of runners.

HEART RATE

The intensity of a cardiovascular workout can be controlled by varying the terrain (uphill or flat) and the amount of resistance. Competitive athletes as well as the serious fitness buff often acquire a special set of training wheels and/or bearings to increase resistance and make the muscles work harder during training practice. If striding poles are used, the upper body receives a better workout as well, increasing the aerobic benefit as well as toning the upper body muscles.

BLOOD PRESSURE

Your heart pumps blood. That's all. About 1.25 times per second, 180,000 times a day, almost 40 million times a year. The heart is fairly simple by design: four muscular chambers, five inches long, three and one-half inches wide, and weighing less than one pound. But notwithstanding its simplicity, its role in your life is vital.[16]

Each time the heart beats, it supplies oxygenated blood and nutrients to your body. The heart's pumping efforts depend on the arteries. When the arteries are dilated and free of cholesterol deposits on the walls, the heart is more efficient and pumps less, thus placing less pressure on the arterial walls. However, the opposite is true as well. If the arteries are constricted or the area of blood passage has decreased, the heart pumps blood at a higher rate, putting more pressure on the arterial wall. This is referred to as high blood pressure.

While blood pressure will temporarily rise due to exercise, excitement, or anxiety, under normal circumstances, the higher the blood pressure, the greater the risk of atherosclerosis. Whether the rise is due to buildup on the arterial walls or genetic history, the net result is excessive strain exerted throughout the arterial system. Thus the heart must pump harder, eventually increasing in size as any muscle does. In simple terms, it is a measure of how hard your heart has to work to do its job. Like many other things, your heart has a life expectancy. The harder and more often it has to work, the shorter its life becomes — and by extension, so does yours.

Because blood pressure and cholesterol share an intimate relationship, knocking out the contributing factors to either one is doing the same to the other. Are you eating again? Are you hungry? What are you eating? You could not be smoking and reading this book at the same time, could you? Are you under a lot of stress? Are you obsessed with something over which you have no control? Whose life is it? Yours!

DIET

Recommended diets are changing all the time. So is the type of diet. What do you want to do? Lose a lot of weight in a short amount of time? Get healthy overnight? How do you navigate the diet maze? Through awareness, information, and discipline.

Are You Hungry?

To start, eat when you are hungry. We all suffer from *boredom hunger*. We tend to feed our appetite, not our body, when our moods get the better of us. Although sometimes it is impossible to get out from under those ominous clouds of despair, an awareness of why and when you are eating can go a long way toward helping you eat out of "hunger" and for no other reason.

Are Calories So Bad?

With all the talk about losing weight, calories are getting a bad name. Everyone is always trying to burn them. If we did not take in enough calories, we would not be able to move. More often, however, we take in too many, and they are stored as fat. Also of importance is *where* we get the calories we need.

Feeding the Fire

About forty-five percent of an average American's calories are from saturated fats — fats from hamburgers, dairy-based concoctions, and the infamous American breakfast: fried eggs, fried potatoes, bacon, ham, and buttered toast, washed down with milk. All these foods contain saturated fats that often accumulate along the walls of your arteries and platelets, small particles that help our blood clot. Over a lifetime of too much cholesterol coupled with general neglect (too little exercise, high blood pressure, stress, and anxiety), our arterial walls shrink in diameter (arteriosclerosis).[17] I think everyone with a television knows what is likely to happen next — a heart attack, the biggest killer in the world. But worse than heart attacks is that we help the process along.

Indeed, "the mechanization of America, ... [most notably] the invention of the elevator, the motor car, and the television, has reduced the majority of our population to a sedentary lifestyle," said Dr. Albert A. Kattus in 1974, when he was chairman of the Exercise Committee of the American Heart Association. What an irony of our age that this scourge of the human race is largely self-inflicted!

WHAT TO EAT?

Any study of nutrients will give you some idea of the utter complexity in the science of nutrition. To make your car run, for instance, all you have to do is "fill it up," not design the perfect blend of climate, distance, occupant weight, etc. Can you imagine having to do this for your car!?

Getting the "fuel" we need is a fairly simple process, thanks to nature. Although diet extremists may set out to eat a load of "nutrients" to design the perfect diet, their efforts would be futile unless they wanted to live on chemicals through an IV. No, you have to buy food, and

Lacking self-confidence? Just look at what a pair of wheels can do for an ego!

In-line racing is no Saturday stroll. Competition continues to grow.

to check off a list of nutrients is a great way to waste time and money. Overloading on protein is not going to build stronger muscles more quickly — protein cannot be stored. Avoid extremes. There is no ideal diet; if there were, then why are there so many of them?

The fact remains that every one of us has different dietary needs. Some need a little more of this, while others need an extra dash of that. So you will need to employ your doctor's and/or nutritionist's advice, but most of all, use common sense in what your body needs and when it needs it. Following are some guidelines to be aware of.

Protein

Protein should make up about fifteen percent of your caloric intake. Almost everyone is aware that meat contains protein. But meat, especially red meat, also contains saturated fat — the least desirable kind of fat for your body. Although chicken contains less fat than red meat, eating the fatty skin on the chicken neutralizes that fact. Make a habit of trimming the fat off meat, broiling or grilling it, and eating it in smaller portions. You will also find protein in fish, beans, and tofu (soybean curd).

Calcium

Calcium is needed to build strong bones. Although much of the growth potential of bones is lost in our early years, you need to maintain their strength and resiliency. While much of our calcium comes from dairy products, dairy products are also high in saturated (animal) fats. Start eating the "low-fat" varieties of milk and cheese. Low-fat and non-fat yogurt is also a good source.

Carbohydrates

Carbohydrates are tricky. We get them from many sources, some good and some bad. Two types of carbohydrates exist in nature — starches and sugars. Roughly half of your total caloric intake should come from starches. Whole grains such as wheat, rice, barley, oats, dried beans, and potatoes are excellent starches. Unfortunately, Americans consume far too much sugar in the form of highly refined (processed) and sweetened (white/brown/raw sugar, honey, and molasses) foods such as pastries, cakes, chocolate, ice cream, and alcohol. They are devoid of nutrients and roughage, and are the worst kinds of calories you can consume, adding weight to your body and cavities in your teeth.

Fats

Fats are a necessary part of your diet. Too many fats are not. Again, there are two types — the good, or polyunsaturated, and the bad, or saturated. Shall I tell you what we consume more of? Yes, again we eat lots of the bad — about twenty times the recommended amount (four to six grams per day). Saturated fats include most meat fat and dairy products, solid shortening products, as well as coconut oil, cocoa butter, palm oil, and milk. However, there lurks good news on the horizon. Vegetable fats of the polyunsaturated variety are not only considered "good" fats, but they also tend to prevent the rise in the blood cholesterol level caused by eating cholesterol-laden saturated fats. A little food for thought, you might say!

Anaerobic exercise, such as in-line skating, will help strengthen and increase your bone mass. But it needs help. Unfortunately, many dairy products that contain calcium are also high in fat. So buy skim or non-fat milk instead of whole milk. Likewise, low-fat cheeses and yogurt are healthful choices. And lest you forget, broccoli is a great source as well.

In fact, given the American diet, it is difficult to consume too many carbohydrates. Grains, wholesome breads, pasta, beans, and potatoes are all powerful building blocks for a good diet, and also an excellent and vital source of fiber. Fruits (pears, bananas, apples), vegetables (corn, carrots, leafy greens), bran bread and muffins, and oat bran are all considered to be good fiber sources.

Vitamins and Minerals

One reason we have been told, reminded, and chided so much and so often since we were children to eat a balanced diet is because without one, our body does not get all the essential vitamins it needs to continue functioning properly. Fortunately, for most of us, there are vitamin supplements we can take. Minerals are similar to vitamins in that they are essential elements required by our bodies to keep going. However, these are inorganic (non-living) substances, while vitamins are organic, meaning they are produced by plants and animals.

5.
Equipment

● ●

Like purchasing a car, opening a bank account, or buying a VCR, the more thought and research you put into your in-line skate purchase, the greater the likelihood you will be satisfied. If you are brimming with enthusiasm, are enduring another sleepless night, and cannot wait a moment more to get in-line, I urge you to rent some skates for a test roll before you put your money on the counter.

There are several good reasons to rent. First, although this experience is rare, you may not like the sensation or feel of in-line skates. Some people actually feel too free, too "out of bounds" to enjoy the sport. And for some, there is a fear factor. Will I be able to stop? What if I fall? How can I balance on a single line of wheels? These are good and legitimate questions. First, you will be able not only to stop, but also to make turns, skate forward and backward, jump over road obstacles, or just "get down" to some funky skate music. And as for falling? Count on it. But like every sport, there is a right way of doing things and a wrong way. If you fall correctly (face forward), you will get up without a scratch. But fall the wrong way and you may incur one of the more common injuries, a broken tailbone or sprained (or broken) wrist. Regarding balance, posture, and every other perception of difficulty you encounter, your positive attitude and will to learn will knock over all those psychological hurdles. Thus accomplished, you will discover in-lining to be one of the easier sports to learn. Moreover, in-line skates are technologically superior to some roller skates you may be familiar with. Couple that fact with the thirty to forty million in-line skaters anticipated by 1995, and how could you doubt *your* ability?

COST

If ever the phrase "getting what you pay for" holds true, it is in shopping for in-line skates. The industry is growing rapidly, more products are being released all the time, and smart shopping has never been so important.

There is no room for inferior materials, secondhand frames, or cheap wheels and bearings. Considering that what you lace on your two feet allows some people to realize speeds of twenty miles per hour and more, it is essential that your purchase be made confidently, with a trusted salesperson or good friend who knows the sport.

If you insist on quality, you may find yourself experiencing tremors of "sticker shock." Before you faint over the $300 you are about to spend on a full in-line package, including complete safety gear (absolutely essential for someone just starting out), consider what you have spent on other sports/activities of leisure — skiing, tennis, golf, backpacking. The cost is really a bargain when compared to many other recreational activities you enjoy. Speaking of enjoyment, what price can be placed on the thrills and "cloud-soaring" freedom to be experienced while skating in-line!

WHERE TO BUY

Fortunately, due to the furious growth of in-line skating, finding exclusive retailers of in-line equipment in the larger- to medium-sized cities should not be a problem. Check your local yellow pages under the listing(s): "Skating Equipment and Supplies" or "Skating Rinks." Also refer to the In-Line Skating Resource Guide at the end of this book.

Ask a friend who skates for advice. Ask around your workplace. Use word of mouth. If all else fails and you know of no one who owns a pair of in-line skates, find a local skating club in your area. If you still come up short, call the International In-line Skating Association (IISA) or one of the industry publications for assistance. They will be delighted to steer you in the right direction.

THINK TWICE

If common sense is so common, why do so few people seem to have it? If you buy a pair of in-line skates through the JollyThrift catalog or see a pair displayed at a convenience store for $49.95, then you deserve every bit of your investment and not a penny more.

Shop around before you buy. The product lines are expanding, and it will become increasingly difficult to see the technological features, quality of materials, or workmanship. Again, speak to the new products manager at one of the industry magazines (see In-Line Skating Resource Guide). Tell him you are just starting out and need help on where to begin. I *guarantee* that you will not be let down by the industry's willingness to talk with you.

BOOTS

Every component of an in-line skate, from a single ball bearing to a boot lace, is only as good as the quality and fit of your boot. Be a shopper, not a buyer. To that end, use the checklist below to ensure that your purchase is well-considered. *Do not* be a victim of an alluring magazine advertisement for in-line skates. *Do* talk with knowledgeable in-line skaters. Ask them where they purchased their equipment. Are they happy with their skates? *Do* contact the in-line publications for advice.

Beware! Unless you have actually tried and fitted the specific model you intend to buy, you are taking a big risk in buying through the mail. This is particularly true for beginning in-liners. Although the listed price may be hard to beat in a retail store, consider shipping cost, insurance, and guarantees offered, and read the small print. Does the company guarantee your satisfaction? Have you heard of the company before? Has anyone? In the interest of thrift, do not fall victim to dubious claims made by shoddy mail-order houses. There are plenty of unscrupulous people lining up to take your money and run!

The Checklist

- Heel brake on one boot.
- Microadjustable ratchet-style buckle closure at boot cuff (ankle).
- If the boot has buckle closures, make sure they are microadjustable. Microadjustable buckles allow the skater to achieve a more precise fit than nonmicroadjustable buckles. Microadjustable buckles have notched settings for the buckle on the strap; on nonmicroadjustable buckles, the settings for the buckle are usually molded into the side of the boot, and customarily offer only about six different settings. Avoid this technology; it's outdated.

Never lean back on skates! Sprained or broken wrists and bruised tailbones are fairly common with beginning skaters. If you lose control or are out of balance, falling forward, knees and hands first, is the safest way to hit the deck.

The heel brake is among the first techniques a beginning skater learns.

Notice the lacing technique here. By using three individual laces on one boot, you can improve the comfort and fit of your skate. There are no rules — just trial and error until it feels right.

A five-wheel aluminum racing frame. Five-wheeled skates increase stability by distributing the weight across a longer chassis.

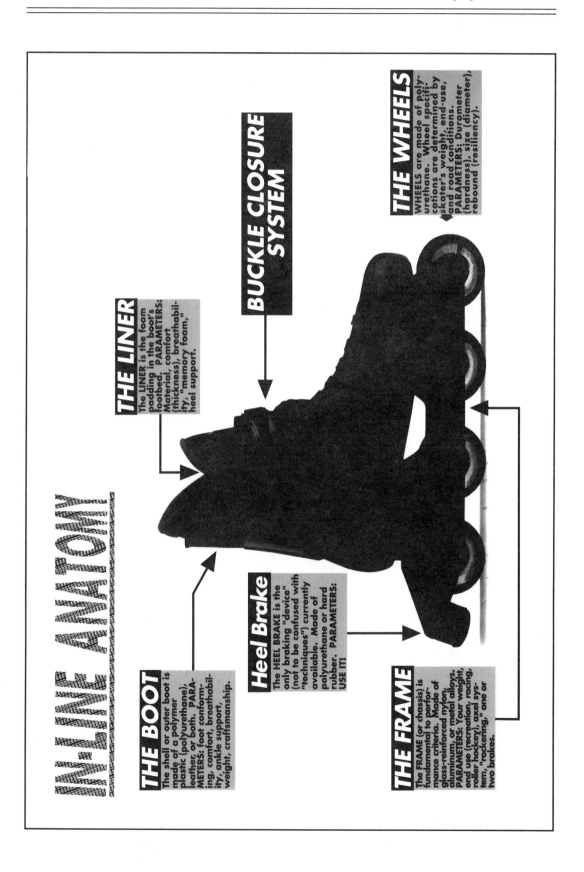

IN-LINE ANATOMY

THE BOOT
The shell or outer boot is made of a polymer plastic (polyurethane), leather, or both. PARAMETERS: foot conforming, comfort, breathability, ankle support, weight, craftsmanship.

THE LINER
The LINER is the foam padding in the boot's footbed. PARAMETERS: Material, comfort (thickness), breathability, "memory foam," heel support.

BUCKLE CLOSURE SYSTEM

THE WHEELS
WHEELS are made of polyurethane. Wheel specifications are determined by skater's weight, end-use, and road conditions. PARAMETERS: Durometer (hardness), size (diameter), rebound (resiliency).

Heel Brake
The HEEL BRAKE is the only braking "device" (not to be confused with "techniques") currently available. Made of polyurethane or hard rubber. PARAMETERS: USE IT!

THE FRAME
The FRAME (or chassis) is fundamental to performance criteria. Made of glass-reinforced nylon, aluminum, or metal alloys. PARAMETERS: Your weight, end use (recreation, racing, roller hockey), axel system, "rockering," one or two brakes.

- "Memory foam" liner to conform to foot for a custom-like fit.
- Tools for removal of wheels.
- Liner is well-made, substantial; generally speaking, the "beefier" the liner, the better (liners break down after prolonged use).
- Boots are comfortable.
- Will the frame design allow you to rocker your wheels and/or shorten or lengthen your wheelbase?
- Do the wheels have an inner hub? An inner hub gives the wheel a stiffer, more solid-feeling ride; some hubs are designed to cool the bearings by circulating air around them.
- Will the frames accommodate wheels larger than 70mm? While smaller wheels are fine for most general-purpose and roller hockey applications, larger wheels will allow you to cover distance more efficiently (see section on wheels).
- What kind of material is the boot constructed of? Generally speaking, polyurethane has a better feel and offers more support than polyethylene or other copolymer plastics.
- What is the frame made of? Is it stiff enough to support your weight and the type of skating you plan on doing without flexing? Grab the frame and squeeze it. If it bends or flexes easily, it is probably not stiff enough.
- Manufacturer's warranty: sixty days or ninety days.
- Warranty information.
- Product documentation.
- Weight.
- Ankle support.

The Fit

Consider the fit of the in-line boot just as you would a pair of walking boots. You will be spending — I hope — a lot of time wearing your skates. An improper fit can quickly take all the fun out of an otherwise delightful activity. If you are not offered a "test roll," acquaint yourself with the feel of the skate before leaving the store. To further illustrate, think of in-line skating as skiing. The skates become the skis, boots, and bindings all in one component. Without a snug fit, "edging" and stopping ability is compromised, and blister formation is probable. The boot should envelop your foot. When standing erect, your toes should either just miss, or barely touch, the front of the liner. Although the likelihood of a *perfect* fit is slim, most people can make minor adjustments through "creative" lacing (i.e., tight and low, loose in the middle, tight and high) and/or buckling the boot. Often, a generic orthotic will cushion a nagging pressure point or fill a minute void quite well. Still, a scant few, like myself, may need to have custom orthotics prescribed. In many of the second- and third-generation designs, the boot is fitted with buckles that add further support to the ankle. Power straps may be purchased if you feel that your boots do not provide adequate ankle support.

When fitting your boots, make sure you are wearing the appropriate socks. Ideally, the skater should be wearing as little "sock" as possible. Thorlo® and Double-Lay-R® both make thin socks specifically for skating. Due to the constant and unavoidable movement of the foot inside the boot, wearing two socks can often lead to sock bunching and blistering. The goal is

Leather racing boots with power straps fastened around the boot to increase ankle stability. Although leather boots are often lighter and more comfortable, they do not provide as much foot support as does the boot with a polyurethane shell.

The "Eddy Matzger Special." Copyright 1992 and courtesy of Team Karim.

In-line skates by Bauer.

Above, the Raps High Top with a Marathon roller chassis. Below, the Raps High Top with the Olympic Ice Racer. Courtesy of Team Karim.

to keep your feet cool and dry. If you do not and your feet are tender, you will likely end up with hot spots and/or blisters. Ultimately, your own experience should determine your choice of footwear.

Fitting Racing Boots

If speed is what you need, then you will want to consider purchasing a pair of racing boots. Generally, racing boots are made of leather or another pliable material and are fitted more snugly than recreational skate boots. Therefore, it becomes absolutely critical to fit the boot properly. Make sure that there is enough room in the toe box. If the toes are compressed or squeezed, you will likely have foot discomfort at best and further physical ailments at worst.

If you have never had your feet examined by a podiatrist (foot doctor), it is wise to do so prior to fitting an expensive pair of boots. The doctor can determine whether an internal orthotic may increase your comfort as well as your posture and circulation.

Modern Evolution of the Boot and Its Future

In the early 1980s when Scott Olson and his brothers developed the first Rollerblade® in-line skate, early efforts were focused on the frame and wheel components. The design of the boot was largely an afterthought. It showed, or rather, felt! After a few hours of skating, your feet became uncomfortable. But times have changed and manufacturers — including Scott Olson and company — are now putting enormous resources into treating the foot with tender loving care. In fact, Maska U.S., Inc., an in-line skate manufacturer and maker/distributor of CCM hockey skates, has teamed up with Reebok® and developed the first Reebok Pump™ in-line skate. Indeed, many experts within the industry view in-line skates as the latest in *footwear*. Are Nike® and Reebok® far from launching their own in-line designs? It's a safe bet.

THE WHEELS
Wheels — 3, 4, 5

In-line frames are usually configured with three-, four-, or five-wheeled systems. Some of the smaller sizes in recreational skates may come with frames that only accommodate three wheels. This is due to the fact that the smaller (and shorter) boot cannot physically accommodate a frame large enough to hold four wheels. Three-wheel skates are less stable (shorter wheelbase) and slower (less support surface, more stress on fewer bearings) than their four-wheeled counterparts.

Five-wheeled skates have longer wheelbases, which increase stability at high speeds and — due to the increased stroke friction provided by the added wheel — have increased lateral traction, which means a skater can push harder to the side without slipping. This simply means a skater will be getting added power from every stroke.

Although I have seen in-line skaters wearing six-wheeled skates, as of yet there appears to be no significant racing advantage. Still, some racers in the Northwest find that a six-wheel frame is desirable for training on slick roads, as they provide greater lateral traction.

Size or Diameter

Wheel size is measured in millimeters. Sizes range from about 67mm for children's sizes to 80mm-plus for competitive racers. The size of the wheel is expressed by measuring the outside diameter of the wheel, referred to as the "OD" of a wheel.

Selecting the appropriate size is a function of the type of in-line skating (recreation, speed, slalom, in-line hockey) you plan on doing.

Durometer

A durometer is actually an instrument used for measuring the hardness of polyurethane, the primary material used in skating wheels. The hardness of in-line wheels is measured on the "A" scale, which reflects increasing hardness. As the number increases, so too does the wheel's hardness. Conversely, as the number decreases, the wheel's polyurethane becomes softer. The current market range is between 74A and 93A. Softer wheels have greater traction, cornering, and shock absorption. Thus, they are best suited to rough surfaces, areas with tight turns, or wet or damp pavement. High durometer wheels should be used on smoother surfaces, for heavier people, and for longer wear. The weight of the skater and the profile of the skating terrain (smooth asphalt, rutted concrete, etc.) are the factors used to determine the appropriate durometer. However, without considering the weight of the skater, determining the appropriate durometer is a moot point.

Rebound

Rebound is the amount of energy put into the wheel, which is then returned, not absorbed, by its source of energy. Just recall the last time you bounced a basketball on the floor. The action of the basketball springing back to you is known as rebound. If the rebound in in-line skate wheels is high, they will be faster and more lively and require less energy than low rebound wheels. Low rebound wheels make you work harder. Skaters looking to intensify their training will sometimes wear low rebound wheels.

Core

A wheel's core is fundamental to the entire wheel, as everything else is built upon the core. The core's shape, density, and material affect performance characteristics such as stability, cornering, and safety. Its design is also often critical to the cooling of the bearing, as some cores are designed to circulate air around the bearing. Given the speed, terrain, and weight placed upon the core assembly, it is essential that it can manage heat build-up and intense stress without "blowing out."

Profile

The profile of the wheel surrounding the core ranges from a small radius, or pointed, wheel to a large radius, or more blunt, wheel. The profile affects speed, cornering, and wear. A large radius wheel has a larger "footprint" and affords better cornering, but has a higher rolling resistance. Conversely, a small radius wheel has less surface resistance for achieving higher speeds.

Colors

What do all of the bright pretty colors mean? Not a thing, but the bright colors make in-line skating even more fun for some people. There are colors available for everyone's style!

A racing skate adjusted for increased maneuverability.

LABEDA in-line wheels.

Wheels in the making. A novel new wheel design. Courtesy of Revolution Inline.

*Blasting through the steeplechase at ROLLERMANIA,
Golden Gate Park, San Francisco.*

THE WHEEL

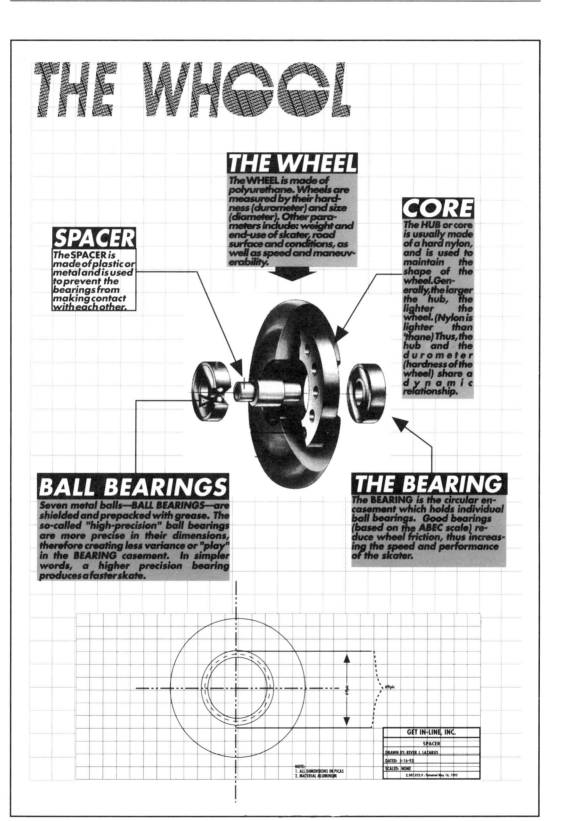

THE WHEEL

The WHEEL is made of polyurethane. Wheels are measured by their hardness (durometer) and size (diameter). Other parameters include: weight and end-use of skater, road surface and conditions, as well as speed and maneuverability.

CORE

The HUB or core is usually made of a hard nylon, and is used to maintain the shape of the wheel. Generally, the larger the hub, the lighter the wheel. (Nylon is lighter than 'thane) Thus, the hub and the durometer (hardness of the wheel) share a dynamic relationship.

SPACER

The SPACER is made of plastic or metal and is used to prevent the bearings from making contact with each other.

BALL BEARINGS

Seven metal balls—BALL BEARINGS—are shielded and prepacked with grease. The so-called "high-precision" ball bearings are more precise in their dimensions, therefore creating less variance or "play" in the BEARING casement. In simpler words, a higher precision bearing produces a faster skate.

THE BEARING

The BEARING is the circular encasement which holds individual ball bearings. Good bearings (based on the ABEC scale) reduce wheel friction, thus increasing the speed and performance of the skater.

69pic

GET IN-LINE, INC.

SPACER

DRAWN BY: RIVER J. LAZARUS

DATED: 5-16-93

SCALED: NONE

NOTE:
1. ALL DIMENSIONS IN PICAS
2. MATERIAL ALUMINUM

Wheel Selection

As you can surmise, your wheel choice should be determined by your skating ability, surface conditions, body weight, and in-line skating goals.

Bearings and Matters of Resistance

It takes effort to skate. Every effort you make to move from a place of rest has several elements working against it. First, there is gravity. Gravity is the force that causes things to fall to the ground and stay there. Each time a leg is lifted or an arm is swung forward, the force of gravity exerts itself by "pulling" at our vertical/lateral movement.

Second, the skater has to manage air resistance. When you walk into a strong head wind, you experience air resistance working its might. The world has spent hundreds of billions of dollars attempting to tame this force through aerodynamic technology in virtually every industry so affected; most notably, the auto industry.

As the distance between world-class athletes is measurable only in hundredths of seconds, the science of aerodynamics is employed to maximize the speed and efficiency of downhill skiers through wind-cutting body position and form-fitting racing suits. Competitive in-liners, too, reduce their drag by wearing body-hugging uniforms and employing streamlined body positions.

Finally, there is resistance. Since the basic wheel was invented, it has gone through a major evolution to overcome surface friction. The first wheelbarrow used an axle, while improved efficiency in automobiles is due in large part to the air-inflated tire.

Enter the ball and bearing. To the layman, it is nothing more than so many tiny metal marbles encased in a metal doughnut. But as you dissect this device, which is no wider than a nickel, you reveal its vital entrails. Most bearings have steel shields that protect the innards of the bearing unit. Remove the shield and you will find a lubricant — usually grease or oil — that keeps things turning smoothly. Should dirt or sand find their way into the bearing, the precision surfaces inside the bearing will wear dramatically. The bearing will lose its silky feel and will start to roll noisily. As mechanical wear increases, so, too, will rolling resistance and "play" within the bearing. This will cause increased side-to-side movement of the wheel and, finally, vibration. In extreme cases, this vibration may cause diminished control at higher speeds.

Greased bearings will last longer than oiled bearings because grease is thicker and protects better. However, some racers will strip the grease out of their bearings and use a light oil for racing. Lighter oils allow the bearings to spin more freely than a heavy grease (less resistance), but bearing life is reduced.

The AB(E)C's of Bearings

The ABEC in the rating code of bearings tends to make the whole system more complicated than it needs to be. ABEC simply stands for Annular Bearing Engineering Council. The bearings themselves are rated on a scale of 1 to 9, with the acronym ABEC placed in front of the number. Bearings rated by the Council are referred to as *precision bearings*. Bearings not rated by the ABEC receive the plain vanilla designation of *semi-precision* or *unground precision*. For instance, a rating of 1, that is ABEC-1, is the lowest rating and thus the lowest *tolerance* established by the ABEC. The other is that only the odd numbers are used — 1, 3, 5, 7, and 9. While 1's and 3's are considered "commercial" grade, 5's and 7's are called "super precision." If you have ever had too much chocolate in a chocolate chip cookie to the point that it was almost *too good*, you can apply that same logic to a bearing rated at ABEC-9.

Donnie Sinnar jumps head over heels for Team Courtesy of Los Altos, California.

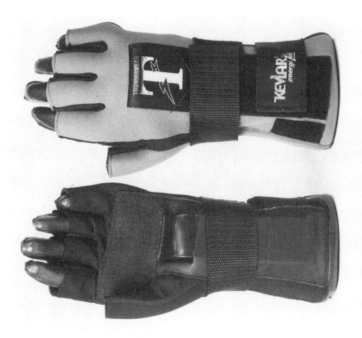

When falling, your hands and wrists are the first to make contact. Protect them.
Shown are Thunderwear® skate gloves with Kevlar palms and built-in wrist guards.
Courtesy of Thunderwear®.

Protect your knees with knee guards. These are Thunderwear knee pads.

There is nothing uncool about protecting your head and eyes when skating.

Tolerance

Due to the advances in manufacturing, the difference between ABEC-1 and ABEC-3 is negligible. Until you upgrade from ABEC-1 to ABEC-5 or ABEC-7, the tolerance level and the cost are not commensurate with performance. Likewise, ABEC-5 bearings have become difficult to find because their performance is so indiscernible from ABEC-7. High ABEC-number bearings lose their rated degrees of precision dramatically when contaminants find their way into the bearing. Therefore, an ABEC-1 should be the ideal outdoor bearing, as it allows minor levels of contamination to exist inside the bearing. In a lower ABEC bearing, there is more room between the moving parts (lower tolerances), so contaminants don't have to grind themselves room within the bearing. Higher ABEC bearings (say, 5 and up) should really only be used indoors as their superior-precision qualities go right out the window as soon as they are contaminated.

The poor tolerance of non-precision bearings can take the fun out of skating. Imagine riding a bicycle with two flat tires. At greater rpm's (revolutions per minute), non-precision bearings tend to wobble. At high speeds this feels like vibration. Not only does this cause the wheels to wear unevenly, but overall performance will take a drastic turn for the worse.

Remember the cookie with too many chocolate chips? ABEC-7, the top of the line, super-precision bearings discussed here have a performance envelope of 50,000 rpm — or a ground speed of some 400 miles per hour![18] Tighten your helmet and put us all to shame!

MAINTENANCE
Wheels
REPOSITIONING AND ROTATING

There are essentially two steps in what is commonly referred to as "rotating" your wheels. The first step is repositioning them; the second, actually rotating them. Before you begin, you will need an Allen wrench and an open-end wrench. Both of these tools are typically included with your skate purchase. If not, they can be purchased separately at a skate shop.

When repositioning the wheels, think of "cycling" from one end of the skate to the other. First, remove the front wheel and move it to the back. Then replace each wheel forward one wheel length. For example, in repositioning a five-wheel racing skate, wheel one is moved to wheel position five, wheel five is moved to position four, and so on. (See illustration.)

In addition to repositioning (moving the front wheel to the rear position, etc.), you will need to rotate each wheel. "Rotating" a wheel means turning the wheel on its vertical axis (as if you were spinning a top) so that the side that is currently facing outward is now facing inward. To remain consistent and maintain smooth performance, rotate each wheel so that the edge with the least amount of wear is facing inward and the manufacturer's name imprint on each wheel is facing in the same direction. While the wheels are off the frame, wipe off dirt and road grease. When placing each wheel back on the frame, tighten each bolt securely, but not too tight. It is important to be consistent when tightening each wheel so that they all spin uniformly. Make small adjustments until they do.

Some skates come with what is called a "rockerable" frame. The rockering feature allows you to create a curved wheel-line (like an ice hockey blade) as opposed to an even one, which is flat. The adjustment provides more maneuverability for quick turns and pivots to perform figure or dance skating. To adjust the rocker, remove your middle wheels (only the single middle wheel from a three-wheeled unit) and locate the holes where the bolts are inserted. Remove the frame spacing insert in the holes of the wheel cavity of the frame. Turn them upside down. Both frame spacer openings must be arranged identically so that the axle will fit through.

To return the wheel base to a flat position, simply reverse this process. Many frames allow you to extend or shorten the wheel base (the total length the wheels are aligned). A longer wheel base redistributes your weight for added stability and speed. A shorter wheel base, although not as fast or as stable, allows for a greater range of maneuverability — quicker turns and pivots.

Keep in mind that new innovations are continually entering the marketplace. Refer to the instructions for your own skates for specific tuning and maintenance advice.

Bearings

If your push and glide is not what it used to be, is not the free flowing experience it should be — it may be time to give your bearings a little TLC. The best method of determining if your bearings need a cleaning is to spin the wheels. If they feel gritty, it's time to get to work.

NOTE: For the uninitiated, cleaning and re-lubricating your bearings can be a filthy undertaking indeed. If you have no desire to know your in-lines on such an intimate level, most full-service skate shops offer wheel and bearing tune-ups. It's really up to you. I suggest you go through the process at least once so you become familiar with how your skates work.

1. The bearing assembly is encased within the center of each wheel. Begin by removing each wheel. (Bearing cleaning is best done during the wheel repositioning/rotating process, as the wheels are off the frame at this point anyway.)

2. Remove (pop out) each bearing with the tool supplied by the manufacturer. A flat head bolt will work also.

3. Place the bearing on several layers of newspaper, paper towels, or a rag you are willing to part with.

4. Apply a solvent such as WD-40™ to the exposed bearings. Wash your hands. Wait about half an hour and turn the bearings over. Apply the solvent again. Wait half an hour. (Be sure you do this step in a well-ventilated area. The solvent produces noxious fumes.)

5. With a clean rag or paper towel, remove the excess dirt and grime from each bearing.

6. Apply a drop of bearing oil to each bearing. After the oil has passed, wipe away the excess oil and, holding with your thumb and forefinger, spin the bearing around its axis.

7. Place one bearing in the wheel, insert the spacer, and pop the other bearing into the wheel. You're sandwiching the spacer inside the wheel between the two bearings.

8. Tighten the bolts.

PROTECTIVE GEAR
Wrist Guards

When you take a spill while in-line skating — and you will fall — it is essential that you protect your palms from cuts and abrasions and your wrists from sprains. Do you remember the last time you took an unplanned trip over a curb? What was the first part of your body to hit the deck? More than likely, your hands. When your body senses that it is off balance, a message is sent to your brain to throw out your hands to brace the fall. Wrist guards do such an outstanding job at protecting your hands from cuts, bruises, road burns, and embedded gravel, and your wrists from sprains and breaks, that is just plain dumb not to wear them at all times. When shopping for wrist guards, look for an in-built plastic support bar that runs from your palm to your wrist.

You are most likely to "lock up" with other skaters or take a fall in the first few hundred yards of a race. Give yourself space until the pack breaks apart.

SEPTEMBER 1992   PAGE 7

SPEEDSKATING TIMES

Dear Editor:
My name is Wendy. I am a registered nurse in an intensive care unit at one of the top university medical centers in the country. I am also an avid inline speedskater.

This past Saturday was one that has left a lasting impression on me. Admitted to one of our intensive care units was an individual who has suffered massive head injuries while inline skating. This person did not have a helmet, lacked protective gear and had no brakes on his skates. In spite of his lack of protection, he went down a steep hill with fellow skaters; however, he was unable to stop or control his speed. His life and the lives of his family will never be the same. Head injuries have very serious consequences. If he had on a helmet and protective gear, perhaps he would be home with his family now and not fighting for his life in our intensive care unit.

Please encourage your readers who are inline skaters to be sensible. It is a matter of life or death.

Yours thru skating,
Wendy, Southern California

Courtesy of Speedskating Times, 1992.

Knee Pads and Elbow Pads

The human knee and elbow are two of the most fragile and poorly designed parts of the human anatomy. Fortunately, in-line skating is among the lowest impact sports. Still, your elbows and knees need protection against the shock of a fall. In selecting knee and elbow protection, look for a combination of a padded cushion inside a hard plastic shell. Both knee and elbow pads should fit snugly, but should afford comfortable flexing — particularly at the knee. Before you make a purchase, check the comfort level by walking around the store. Try a few practice squats. Also, be aware that Velcro® straps tend to offer more precise adjustments than do traditional elastic straps.

Helmet

A helmet messes up your hair. It adds weight to your body. And "worst" of all, it does not look "cool." There is no escaping the fact that there is something artificial strapped to your head.

Given nine lives like our feline friends, I would not think twice about tossing the helmet to the side and letting the free flow of air rush through my hair. But we are mortal, and I fear it is going to take a myriad of tragic examples for in-liners to be affected enough to don their headgear consistently, whether strolling along a sidewalk or jamming down the highway. It's your choice. You make it. And you live or die with it!

Whistle

Cars have horns. Dogs bark. You should have a whistle.

Try something — it will be fun. At 12:30 p.m., go to the business district in your community. Find the busiest intersection and watch. Just watch and start counting every close call, near miss, and near hit. Listen for every horn. Note the respect — or lack thereof — drivers give pedestrians. Pay particular attention to drivers turning right on a red light, nudging through pedestrians like they were so many eddies of debris. Now look back down the street. Have you seen a subcompact playing "chicken" with a bus yet? Every day many enter battle just to move their bodies from point A to point B. And make no mistake, it is battle. The stress is palpable. Time is precious, there is money to be made, and everyone is in the way. Even Lee Iacocca, former chairman of Chrysler, was fond of saying, "In this business you either lead, follow, or get out of the way." So, if you must skate through high traffic areas — and many in-liners love to — hang a whistle around your neck.

CLOTHING

Both the weather and the type of skating you are doing will help determine what you wear. For warm weather recreational skating, shorts and a T-shirt are fine. Remember, properly worn safety gear is your shield; your clothes are not. For cold weather, layering your clothes is most practical. A basic three-layer outfit consists of a primary fleece or "wicking" layer to remove the wetness from your body, a secondary insulating cotton layer, and a lightweight windbreaker on top. *Do not* attempt to skate in the rain, the snow, or extremely cold, icy conditions.

BACKPACKS AND EQUIPMENT CARRIERS

You may find "porta-luggage" to be unnecessary, but lest you find out the hard way, in-line preparedness is an important consideration. If you plan on a skate any longer than an hour, consider the following:

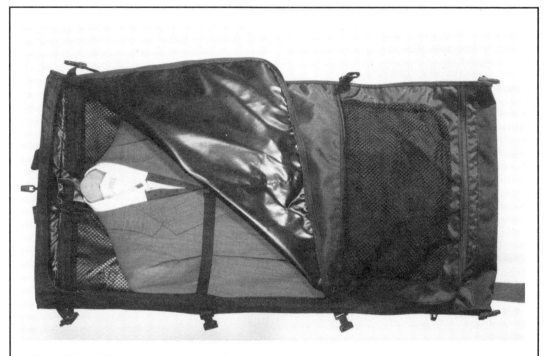

The ENRGE™ Sports Backrider™ is a great way to tote clothing, shoes, and sundries for commuting on your in-line skates to work. Courtesy of ENRGE Sports, Inc.

These Bladelights emit a bright, focusable light in front of the skates, improving ability to see and be seen. Courtesy of Paragon Racing Products.

- No matter how long you plan to be out, always have a driver's license or an official state identification card with you. This can be stashed in between your boot and socks, or tucked somewhere underneath your pant wear.

- Keys. The house and/or car key is all you need. Keep it simple. Single keys fit and loop nicely in the laces of your skates.

- Depending on the climate and terrain, you may want to carry some water and high-energy snack food. A Snickers bar is okay; trail mix and fruit are better.

- Sunglasses or clear safety goggles. This is determined by climate and terrain. Highway/distance skaters should wear eye protection. A speck of sand or a fly can send you into a tailspin — literally!

- The rest is up to you. Chapstick™ is great. Sun block? Bandanna? A hand towel or sweatband is good for sopping up perspiration.

- Leave the Walkman™ at home. Your eyes and ears are your best defense against the many obstacles you may encounter while skating. If you must wear headphones, make sure that you are in a secure area — parking lot, blocked road, etc. — free from traffic. By "traffic" I mean anything that independently moves about your skating area — people, motor vehicles, pigeons, other skaters, and so on.

JEWELRY

There are two reasons not to wear a watch or jewelry while skating — the risks of loss and further contributing to injuries. If you do wear a watch, wear it loosely and preferably with a plastic or Velcro® band, for two reasons. If the watch gets caught on something, the strap will break free before your wrist does. Also, as your blood pressure rises due to exertion, your wrist may expand enough to make a tight band uncomfortable.

6.
Strength and Flexibility

A healthy body that is fueled with wholesome foods, supported by strong bones and muscles, and resistant to disease is less apt to sustain permanent injury in a fall. It is also likely to heal much quicker if there is an injury. This chapter will show you how to be best prepared physically for in-line skating.

GETTING READY

Find an area free of traffic and distractions. A patch of grass or an old towel over concrete is fine. It is best to complete your stretching routine with your skates off, as they tend to get in the way.

Breathing

Breathe as you stretch. If you grit your teeth and hold your breath, you block the flow of oxygen (fuel) to your body. If a particular position is obstructing your breathing, adjust your body position until you are relaxed and breathing normally again.

Don't Overdo It

Whenever you over-stretch, you send a message to the body to contract the muscle in order to protect it from injury, as our bodies believe relaxed muscles are more prone to injury. Holding a stretch beyond your maximum flexibility or bouncing a stretch strains the muscle and activates what is called the "stretch reflex." It hurts, and damages the muscle by tearing microscopic muscle fibers. Just as a scar is created when you cut yourself, the muscle scars when it is damaged. Ultimately, elasticity is reduced and your muscle becomes tight and sore. Moreover, subsequent stretching becomes a loathsome experience, when in fact it should relax you and allow blood to reach your farthest extremities.

Many of us have been misguided by the time-worn myth, "No pain, no gain." In stretching, nothing could be further from the truth. Proper stretching is not painful. Pain, in fact, should tell you something is wrong with your stretching technique or may indicate a previously damaged muscle or tendon. In such cases, do not hesitate to see your doctor.

Most stretches should be held for thirty seconds and then can be gradually increased to sixty seconds.

HEAD ROLLS

Assume a standing position with your arms at your sides. Roll your head around your chest, shoulders, and back several times in both directions. Now flex your head forward by dropping your chin downward as far as possible.

Next, extend your head as far backward as possible. This exercise improves neck flexibility and also helps to firm the muscles in front of the neck.

LEGS, CALVES, AND ACHILLES TENDONS

These stretches will increase the flexibility and energy in your legs.

To stretch the calf, stand a small distance from a wall or post and lean into it with your forearms. Your head should rest on your hands. Bend one leg and place your foot on the ground in front of you, extending the other leg straight behind you. Slowly move the hips forward, keeping your lower back flat. It is essential to keep the heel of the back leg firmly planted on the ground with your toes slightly turned as you hold the stretch. Do two sets and repeat with the other leg.

To stretch the top of the foot and shin, maintain the same position against the post, bend both knees, and dip your body downward. Keep your front foot flat on the ground while flexing the top of the back toe into the ground. Because the small muscle of the shin is rarely used, you may feel tightness there after a day of striding up hills.

For the calf and Achilles tendon, lower the hips downward as you bend the knee slightly. The back remains flat. Your back foot should be slightly toed-in. The heel remains firmly planted on the ground. Be careful when stretching the Achilles tendon, as it only needs a slight stretch. Do two sets and repeat with the other leg.

The stretch shown here demonstrates an effective method of stretching the Achilles tendon and the back of the calf. For safety, try to find a curb with a telephone pole or parking meter next to it. You will want something to hold onto should you lose your balance. Repeat this step twice on each leg.

QUADRICEPS AND HAMSTRING
Standing Stretches

Assume a bent-knee position with your heels flat on the ground, toes pointed straight ahead, and feet about shoulder-width apart.

In this position, you are tightening the quadriceps and relaxing the hamstrings. As you hold this bent-knee position, notice the difference between the front of the thigh and the back of the thigh. The quadriceps (front) should be firm and tight while the hamstrings (back) should feel soft and relaxed.

Sitting Stretch for the Quadriceps

Sit with your right leg bent and your right heel just to the outside of your right hip. Your left leg is straight out in front of you.

In this position, your foot should be extended back with the ankle flexed. If your ankle is tight, move the foot just enough to the side to lessen the tension. Try not to let the foot flare out to the side in this position. By keeping your foot pointed straight back, you remove the stress on the inside of your knee. The more your foot flares to the side, the more stress is exerted on your knee. Remember, your knee is relatively fragile.

Now, slowly lean straight back until you feel mild tension. Use your hands for balance and support.

Do not let your knee come up from the ground. This indicates that you are over-stretching. Switch legs. Do two sets.

Preparing for racing action, stretching the hamstring.

Stretching the quadriceps. Be careful not to place too much stress on the bent leg.

*Stretch the upper body and spinal column. Taking the time to stretch properly
will go a long way toward preventing spinal injury.*

Sitting Stretch for the Hamstring

Sit with your right leg straight and the sole of your left foot slightly touching the inside of the right thigh. You are now in a straight-leg, bent-knee position. Slowly bend forward from the hips toward the foot of the straight leg until you feel tension. After the tension has diminished, bend a bit more and hold.

During this stretch, keep the foot of your straight leg upright, relaxing the ankle and toes. Be sure that the quadriceps is relaxed during this stretch. If you cannot easily reach your feet, use a towel to help you stretch.

HIPS, HAMSTRINGS, AND GROIN

To stretch the muscle in front of the hip, move one leg forward until the knee of the forward leg is directly over the ankle. Rest your other knee on the ground. Without changing the position of the knee on the ground or the front foot, slowly lower the front of your hip downward. You should feel this stretch in the front of the hip and perhaps in the hamstring and groin, depending on your current flexibility.

Groin

Place the soles of your feet together and hold your toes. Gently pull yourself forward, bending from the hips, until you feel a little tension in your groin. Try to place your elbows on the outside of your legs and slowly bend the spine downward. Do not bounce. Do two sets and remember to breathe.

An alternative method, if you have trouble balancing, is to sit against a wall or couch. With your back straight and the soles of your feet together, use your hands to push gently downward on the inside of your thighs. *Do not* push on your knees! Push until you feel a little tension and hold. Do two sets.

UPPER BODY

This stretch is excellent for stretching the muscles from your side along the arms to the hips. I refer to it as the *full body stretch.*

Stand with your feet together and toes pointed straight ahead. Place both hands over your head and clasp them together. Now, as though you are reaching for something high above you, slowly bend to the right. Form is critical in order to get maximum benefit from this stretch.

Your head should remain level and eyes should be focused straight ahead. Pick out an object in the room and don't let your eyes veer from it. Do two sets on both sides of your body. For those with weak backs, instead of extending both hands in the air, use one to support your hip. Every other position and movement remains the same.

UPPER LEG

From a sitting position with one leg extended straight out, slowly bring your bent knee inward as one unit to your chest. Pull it forward until you feel a gentle stretch in the back of your upper leg. You may want to perform this stretch while you rest your back against a wall or on the back of a couch. Hold for twenty seconds. Repeat.

FEET AND ANKLES

Our feet are precious. They bear the weight of our bodies for a lifetime, but they need some special attention. Here is a series of stretches that will leave your feet and ankles feeling rejuvenated.

Lie flat on your back (this is great to do before you get out of bed in the morning) and extend your toes as far as they will go. Imagine reaching for a one hundred dollar bill that you almost have. You should feel light tension across the top of your feet.

While sitting up, rotate your ankles clockwise and counter-clockwise through a complete circle of motion with slight resistance provided by your hand. This motion helps to stretch tight ligaments and tendons. Repeat ten to twenty times in each direction.

Next, use your fingers to pull your toes gently toward you, to stretch the top of the foot and tendons.

Now pull the toes in the opposite direction to stretch the upper tendons of the foot. Hold each stretch for ten seconds and repeat three times.

Finally, with the flat part of your fist, in rapid succession gently strike along the sole of the foot, moving vigorously from heel to toe. Repeat on the other foot.

CONCLUSION

Every human body is unique and may require some additional stretches. You know your body better than anyone else. If you feel tightness somewhere, do what feels right — slowly and with no bouncing.

Your muscles need to wake up just as you do. A full stretching routine should be done before and after each roll. Neglecting a proper stretch and warm-up routine is a frequent cause of *avoidable* injury.

Stretching achieves a number of things. Primarily, of course, a series of stretches following the proper technique reduces muscle tension, increases the range of motion, and prevents injury. A strong, stretched muscle resists the stress of a fall better than a strong, tight muscle does.

PROFILE: JON LOWDEN

Jon Lowden bought his first pair of in-line skates in 1985. Instantly hooked on the activity, Lowden skated Manhattan streets with a vengeance, blazing through its noontime bustle, dodging taxis, and putting a look of "stunned disbelief" on the faces of pedestrians.

By 1990 he had skated to prominence, becoming one of the country's premier distance racers. People noticed. Among them was John Winsor, President of the Colorado-based Sports and Fitness Publishing, who approached Lowden with an offer to edit his recent upstart, *InLine* magazine. He tentatively accepted.

Although an in-line authority, Lowden lacked *any* editorial skills. But he proved himself up to the challenge. Both as storyteller and in-line skating advocate, Lowden engages his reader in his topic. He is, in F. Scott Fitzgerald's words, "incurably honest." And although his opinions may occasionally disillusion and often challenge the sensibilities of his readers, in the end Jon wants to talk about "the real deal."

Author: In response to some of your earlier editorial for the magazine, you have been described by readers as "immature," "irresponsible," "hypocritical," "belligerent," and "insensitive." You strike a contentious chord with your readers. Is this intentional? Does it stem from your strong conventions about the sport, or is it just to sell magazines?

Lowden: No, I'd have to say it's *not* just to sell magazines. If I *only* wanted to sell magazines, I'd concentrate more on putting out something a lot more mainstream … something that would appeal to the mommies and daddies out there who are buying their children skates.

Jon Lowden, Editor, InLine *magazine. Photo copyright 1992 Rod Walker.*

A: As opposed to?

L: Someone who really enjoys the skating activity, and who isn't skating simply because they have a big butt that they're looking to get rid of. I'm not necessarily interested in people who skate solely to get in shape. Actually, I'm somewhat amazed by the peculiar American phenomenon in which people go to a health club, climb on a Stair Master, and then go home and take elevators up to their apartments. By and large, I don't really care much about those people.

A: In the past several years, we have seen the in-line skating industry soar in overall growth by some 6,000%. Many attribute this phenomenon to the early marketing efforts of Rollerblade®. To what do you attribute this explosive growth?

L: Rollerblade® marketing has definitely helped the sport grow, but my personal feeling is that the skates just sell themselves. I remember when I got my first pair of skates; people would look at my feet and say, "What the h — are those things?" I'd say, "They're the coolest thing ever." I'd skate off and they'd be sold right there. In my experience, it's really been a word of mouth thing. Also, in terms of those people who used conventional, or quad, roller skates, well, all they had to do was try in-lines once to realize that they were faster, lighter, more maneuverable, and easier to skate on than traditionally configured roller skates. The bottom line is simply that in-line skates sell themselves. They're fun and they work.

A: Is in-line skating here to stay? Do you think it is a fad in any sense?

L: For some people, it probably is. Some folks are merely mimicking what their neighbors are doing and may realize that skating is too scary for them, or that their feet hurt, or that — somehow — skating just doesn't work for them. In fact, some of the outrageous growth the industry has experienced is certainly attributable to people who have bought skates but will never really use them. Having said that, I think that the in-line skate has as permanent a future as the bicycle. I honestly believe that. Look, it's simpler, cheaper, easier to maintain, and it's very portable — you can store it in a box. After all — like it or not — we're just coating this planet with pavement. What a great place for in-lines!

A: Although the sport has made significant strides in creating a good relationship in many communities, in-line skaters are still considered a menace throughout much of the country. What needs to happen to change this attitude, if that can be achieved?

L: Well, part of the problem is those beginning skaters who lurch down the sidewalk with arms outstretched like listing drunkards. They're a hazard. I also think another part of that "menace" perception stems from a vestigial holdover of people's perception of skateboarders and those Travolta-types who wore white polyester bell-bottoms and disco-danced on quad skates. For what it's worth, those disco-dudes even scare *me*. But somehow, it seems that having any number or configuration of little rubber wheels under your feet qualifies a person as anarchistic and anti-establishment. I was recently pulled over here in Boulder — probably my sixth or seventh time — for skating down a roomy, beautifully paved road. The bike path was way too clogged with pedestrians and runners and bikes for me, so I figured I'd take my chances on the road. The cop who pulled me over told me — as they all do — that he had pulled me over for my own safety. That's bull — it's the "legal" skating on crowded sidewalks and congested bike paths that is truly hazardous. The police in Boulder are just kowtowing to the drivers who pound their dashboards in frustration because passing a skater safely just added an extra eight seconds to their driving time. When I get out on the road, skating at 20-25 mph right along with traffic, drivers are somehow offended. There's a psychological battle that takes place between motorists and skaters. That ticks me off — I pay road taxes, but I don't have a car, and I don't pollute. Shouldn't that entitle me to some sort of special consideration? The bottom line is that most drivers just don't like sharing the road with skaters.

A: Why? What do you mean?

L: Well, back in the old days, cyclists went through the exact same thing when they were trying to use public roadways alongside motor vehicles. However, in-line skaters have a much greater problem than cyclists because we take up so much more room. The average cyclist uses about 18 inches of the roadway, while skaters use at least six feet, which for all intents and purposes amounts to about a full car lane.

That definitely rankles people. Again, we're dealing with this peculiarly opaque American mentality. We shrink the country — the planet, for that matter — with fax machines, cars, and telephones ... time has become money in our society, and getting things done quickly seems to take precedence over getting things done as healthily, as cleanly, and as joyfully as possible. So we have these two polar philosophies out on the road. People interested in fitness, fun, and taking the time to look around and smell the flowers are doing battle with people who owe thousands of dollars on the vehicles they're sitting in, and who are in this flaming rush to get somewhere as quickly as possible, whether it's around the block or a hundred miles away. They've either got to drive that thing to death to justify the expense of owning it, or rush back to work so that they can continue paying for it. In the world of motor vehicles, time and money are king. Our whole economy — steel, oil, highways, shopping malls — revolves around motor vehicles. It's a vicious cycle, that whole "elevator versus taking the steps" thing. We're reducing the amount of physical labor necessary to our having a "good" day so that we can have more time to eat snacks in front of the TV.

A: Skating safely has received a lot of attention with the likes of the SKATESMART campaign. Is the freedom to choose to wear or not to wear safety equipment more important, or is protecting the uninitiated skater from his or her own lack of experience and ability more important? Where does the responsibility of skating safely begin and where does it end in your view?

L: I think it is a personal choice, like buckling up. I think it's important for people to wear helmets — I almost always wear one — but I don't like to be preached at and I don't like to preach at people. With the exception of kids, people should be allowed to make their own decisions regarding safety equipment. We let people smoke, don't we? Frankly, I think the whole safety thing has been blown out of proportion, thanks in part to the rabid hype of the media. If the news media can't find a big controversy, they're always willing to develop or synthesize one.

When you have six or seven million people doing a challenging recreational activity, you know people are going to get injured. And they are going to get killed. Nobody's freaking out over all the injuries that participation in baseball, basketball, or cycling generate, but the stats indicate that all are more dangerous than skating — check out a National Electronic Injury Survey System (NEISS) report sometime. The NEISS people randomly sample emergency-room data from all over the country, and often you pro-rate the data. In other words, adjust the participation frequency of one sport against the participation frequency of another and you find that skating produces a lot fewer injuries than certain media types would have you believe. There have really been comparatively few injuries and fatalities in skating. Compare the data — proportionately speaking, how many people are killed or seriously injured while cycling every year? Also, most serious skate injuries and fatalities have happened to people who didn't use basic common sense; they bought skates, immediately rolled out of the store and down some huge hill, and wasted themselves. Those same people would probably kill or injure themselves no matter what sport they were doing. The bottom line here is that we need to instill some common sense into our consumers by placing a huge emphasis on point-of-sale education. Just a little bit of prevention is worth a lot. And for the future of the sport, we need to give the media as little as possible to scream about.

A: In-line skating currently has two quasi-governing bodies — USAC/RS (United States Confederation of Roller Skating) and IISA (International In-line Skating Association), both of which, according to many in-line opinion leaders, are preoccupied with policy and saving face, and therefore fail to respond adequately to the concerns of the greater in-line citizenry. Would you comment on this and, also, what needs to happen for this sport to have a single, unified governing body?

L: I agree with what you said — there are a lot of hidden agendas cooking. When I first began here at the magazine — when I was an idealistic jerk, rather than just the jerk that I am now — I asked IISA Executive Director Joe Janasz, "When are Joe and Jane Skater going to have a say, or vote, in what goes on with the IISA?" Well, he hemmed and hawed and said something like, "We're working on it." I'm not holding my breath.

As far as the second part of your question goes, I believe that — from a purely operational standpoint — USAC/RS and IISA should join forces. I think they both have incredible strengths. USAC/RS should develop, govern, and officiate all racing and other competitive events, and IISA should work on the legal, political, and public relations and marketing fronts. Unfortunately, because there is a sort of animosity that exists — not between the two groups per se, but between personalities within those two groups — unification may never take place. I think that both groups suffer from a wee bit of inertia. Finally, I think that when you come right down to it, most skaters don't need any organization. You know, you go out and skate and have fun.

A: That's fine for the recreational skater, but how are the in-line competitors ever to know where they rank nationally, considering that just about anyone with a course and a stopwatch is touting their event as a "National Championship"?

L: Well, obviously the competitive skater does need a governing body, for the very reason you cited. But for consumer girl or consumer guy, they want to know what they get for their $25 IISA membership. They can't even get anyone on the phone over at the IISA! You know, there are an awful lot of skaters out there who need a new set of wheels more than they need a membership in USAC or the IISA.

A: Statistically, ice skating is among the most popular sports of the winter Olympics. Obviously, broadcasting networks know this and always broadcast the main skating events in prime time. Why is it that we only see ice skating every four years?

L: Money plays a major part in it. For whatever reason, the media powers that be have decided that skating is of dubious commercial value. We have the Big Three in American sports — football, baseball, and basketball — and media-generated monies drive all of them. It's interesting to note that no sport that wasn't an American invention — like soccer or cycling, for example — ever makes it onto the tube for any length of time. Why? Are we that close-minded? It would be great to see sports like cycling or in-line racing — which are so simple and beautiful and minimalist — on the tube, but the American public seems to have this obsession with teams and balls. They like to see grown men chasing little balls around. It's unfortunate.

7.
Safety

● ●

AAA (AWARENESS — ANTICIPATION — ACTION)

Most learn-to-drive clinics teach "high aim steering." The theory goes that by casting your vision in the distance, you will see potential traffic and have time to react. When in-line skating, you not only need to "high aim" your vision, but you also must employ the "low aim" technique to be aware, anticipate potential obstacles (i.e., that car may back up, this pavement may be rutted, etc.), and finally act with a plan of escape. Note the word "act," as opposed to "react." If you skate along your merry way, oblivious to the world around you, and a pack of dogs starts chasing you with fangs at the ready, you are apt to panic and "react."

By using the AWARENESS-ANTICIPATION-ACTION method, you will always be prepared, having already "foreseen" the worst case scenario and planned for a method of action and avoidance. Remember, "AAA" is the best way to make yourself lucky.

RULES OF THE ROAD

Be a responsible skater and become aware of your local skating laws. Every community has different laws and ordinances. If your community is somehow limiting your right to enjoy the free outdoors like everyone else, get in contact with the closest club or association in your area. Find out what can be done to change the law while protecting everyone. But please, do not play lawyer with the law officer who has stopped you for "speeding" on your skates.

Local Laws

Every community has local ordinances that in some cases regulate, restrict, or ban skating altogether. Although banning skating is certainly excessive, you will not further any cause to reinstate in-line skating by breaking the law.

Citations

Again, different states have different laws. Most states consider in-line skaters to be pedestrians, thus the most frequent citation, aside from off-limits skating, is in-lining on roads and highways.

UNCOMMON COURTESY

Unfortunately, in-line skating has inherited the rude, caustic stigma of skateboarding. Just when neighborhoods were beginning to breathe a sigh of relief, they see another "invasion" of wheeled maniacs.[19]

The best thing you can do to obliterate that image is to skate mindful that you never were, and still are not, the only person in the world. You also need to realize what you look like when you skate and how that can affect non-skaters (pedestrians, vehicles, etc.) and other skaters.

First, realize that the breadth of full stride is at least six feet. Furthermore, your arms are rapidly swinging up and down. Indeed, to someone getting their first look at an in-line skater, you would look like some sort of flailing monster in pain.[20]

PASSING

This sport is just too young to assume that everyone is working under some unifying safety standard. Therefore, it is important that you always announce your intentions — visually or vocally — when you encounter traffic.

When passing someone head-on, staying to the right is generally preferable. Be sure you make that clear to the approaching party. Call out or lift your arm well in advance of your point of passage.

If you are passing someone from the rear, let him know with a firm, "On your right!"

NIGHT SKATING

In-lining at night adds a new dimension and sensation to the thrill of in-line skating. Beware! The dangers multiply exponentially after sunset. Because visibility is so drastically curtailed, a whole new world of hazards opens up. Potholes, pebbles, parked cars, and curbs may seem to come out of nowhere. Everything in the darkness is camouflaged. Take steps to take care of yourself.

Taking the lead in a 10K race.

If you are going to skate at night, select your course during the daylight and inspect it. Take note of construction areas, dips in the road, blind spots, and dangerous neighborhoods.

Make yourself visible. If you have not noticed already, you will find that nearly all in-line products heavily use day-glow colors. This is more than a marketing gimmick; it makes you more visible to others.

For night skating in particular, apply reflectors to your body. Position them carefully on key areas. Because most cars use low-beam headlights, place your reflectors on the heels of your skates, your rear end, your back, and your helmet. Reflectors come in many forms and colors — stickers, pins, Velcro™, vests, belts, wristbands, and headbands. If you are toting a gear bag, a small flashlight is very useful.

BAILING OUT

If you could only witness your car's brake pads after months of racing to stoplights and braking hard. The bottom line is: something has to give — particularly when you are just starting out in-lining. If you must stop suddenly, do yourself a favor and don't worry about residual damage to your skating components. While equipment can be replaced and your skates brought back up to par, your body is fragile and must be given priority over a set of wheels.

If rolling out of the situation appears to be precarious at best, look for a soft or grassy area to stop. If you do choose to roll onto an unpaved surface, anticipate that your skates are going to slow down — a lot — as every last pound of your body is going to keep going. This is called inertia, but you'll call it scary. Try to keep your weight centered over your heels to prevent your toes from digging into the ground, hence rolling into an involuntary somersault.

You have probably anticipated the last resort — to fall using the proper technique. Do not resist your body's desire to keep going. Depending on the speed at which you enter your "emergency landing," you may need to roll many times to lessen your body's forward momentum.. If you are fit, flexible, and wearing your protective gear, you may get up without a scratch. There is a lifetime of enjoyment to be had with in-line skating, but for all the fun, you have to take safety very seriously.

Finally, when you really must stop immediately but all kinds of obstacles — slick roads, traffic, a hill, or countless other hazardous variables — are giving you second thoughts, remember a few basics.

First, do not *panic*. Our innate panic response forces the body and brain to stiffen and freeze. In studying biology, you may recall the "fight or flight" reaction. This is the body's method of protecting itself. Unfortunately, this standard response sometimes works against us. Indeed, to handle emergency situations deftly, you need to remain collected and be prepared for the worst. In this way, you will be apt to handle the worst situation in the best way possible.[21]

TERRAIN

No other "vehicle" on the road has a greater appreciation for the properties of a road than skaters. Considering that your entire body weight is being supported by a line of wheels no larger than a doughnut, what you skate on is tantamount to what you eat. What other user of the road is as dependent upon or respectful of pavement than the in-line skater? Ruts, cracks, and the ubiquitous pothole are the scars and blemishes of the road, and can upend the oblivious in-liner into the blackness of asphalt. A healthy respect for your skating surface will go a long way toward keeping your body the same.[22]

Concrete and Asphalt

To the motorist, the distinction between asphalt and concrete is negligible. The effect that potholes, cracks, and rifts in the road have on the motorist is usually limited. Not so for the in-line skater. The significant distinction between these surfaces is that while concrete is rigid and thus faster, asphalt is flexible, and thereby slower. Indeed, asphalt's surface is ever flexing to the rays of the sun. The experienced or responsible in-liner is aware of the changing characteristics in the skating environment.

Grass

Packed or worn grass is the best place for the uninitiated or beginning skater to get a "feel" for his skates. Not only will falls be more forgiving on the body, but your rolling (wheel movement) ability will be minimal and easier to control. Further, grass is the best area to look for in an emergency situation, particularly as you are careening out of control in a congested area.

Sidewalks

According to most local laws, sidewalks are designed and designated primarily for pedestrians. If you must use a pedestrian sidewalk at "rush hour," be courteous. Do not stride, but walk on your wheels. There is a product (see In-Line Skating Resource Guide) that "locks" your wheels, which is convenient when entering buildings, malls, and the like.

COPING WITH OBSTACLES

Nobody likes to associate a morose topic with such a "blast" of a sport, but like many fun-filled joys in life, in-line skating has a dark flip side — it can be deadly.

This is not to say that skating is a dangerous sport. Ultimately, if you develop a respect for the sport and your abilities, you will become a safe, courteous, and skilled in-liner. Nevertheless, you must always be aware of the countless, looming obstacles over which you have no control. Cab drivers "punching" through yellow lights. Unmarked dips and rifts in the road. A flock of feeding pigeons (I hate pigeons!) launching headlong for your eyes. And, of course, oblivious drivers, and they are countless, changing course without a care in the world.

Among the most common injuries are road burns (aka "strawberries"), bruises, and lacerations. Injuries range from blisters to the near fatal. Despite in-line skating's thrills and euphoria, complete respect for the sport must never leave you. Make no mistake, if you are out to test fate and pit skin against pavement, your skin will lose every time.

Know your limits, skate defensively using the AAA method, and always look out for the unknown.

OBSTACLE	EFFECT	PLAN
Fault: elevation at a joint or crack.	Depending on your center of gravity, it could feel like running into a wall.	Walk or rock 'n roll.
Blow-up: buckling or shattering of rigid pavement.	At slower speeds, wheels can get caught in ruts.	Step over or stride through at an angle.

OBSTACLE	EFFECT	PLAN
Scaling: peeling of the road surface.	Rough ride.	Bend knees to increase shock absorption.
Edge crack: crack between the point where pavement runs parallel to asphalt.	Depending on width expansion due to climate, these may track your wheels.	Step over or stride through at an angle.
Lane joint crack: separation along the seams between two paving lanes.	Depending on width expansion due to climate, these may track your wheels.	Step over or stride through at an angle.
Channel/rut: channelized depression that develops in the tire tracks of asphalt pavement. Frequently found in truck lanes due to enormous weight of trucks.	Tracking your wheels, although not significantly due to width of channel.	Step out.
Upheaval: localized swelling of the pavement.	Depending on size, could result in anything from a jolt to involuntary "air."	Avoid, or lower your center of gravity by bending knees.[23]
Pothole: ubiquitous, bowl-shaped hole of various sizes in pavement.	Depending on size, could cause serious injury.	Avoid, step, or jump over. *Do not* go through.
Driveways.	Depending on the width of the lip, could trip or jolt.	Stride through at an angle. Step up.
Natural road debris: twigs, pebbles, acorns.	Bumpy.	Decrease speed. Rock 'n roll.
Railroad tracks.	Tracking.	Step out. Stride across at an angle.
Curb (from street level to sidewalk level only).	Trip you head first into the ground.	Avoid. Step and roll.
Pigeons and other bird groups.	A pigeon missile in the face is painful and dirty.	Lower body, bend at the knees, and cross arms in front of head. Beware of "sorties" dropping "ordnance" overhead.

Sandy Snakenberg, instructor and in-line racer, hill training on Mt. Tamalpais, California. Courtesy of Team Karim.

Fly, fly away! Chad Pederson, of Team Courtesy, at just thirteen wows an awestruck crowd.

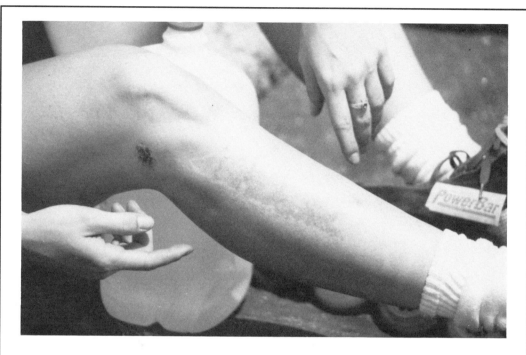

A scar from a road burn, or "strawberry," a common in-line injury.
Clean and cover abrasions of this type to prevent infection.

Greg LeVien and Mike Riddle put on the speed during a training workout in
Berkeley, California. Courtesy of Team Karim.

Taking a look.

*Camp Rollerblade® instructor demonstrates a power brake,
a very effective way of stopping quickly and under control.*

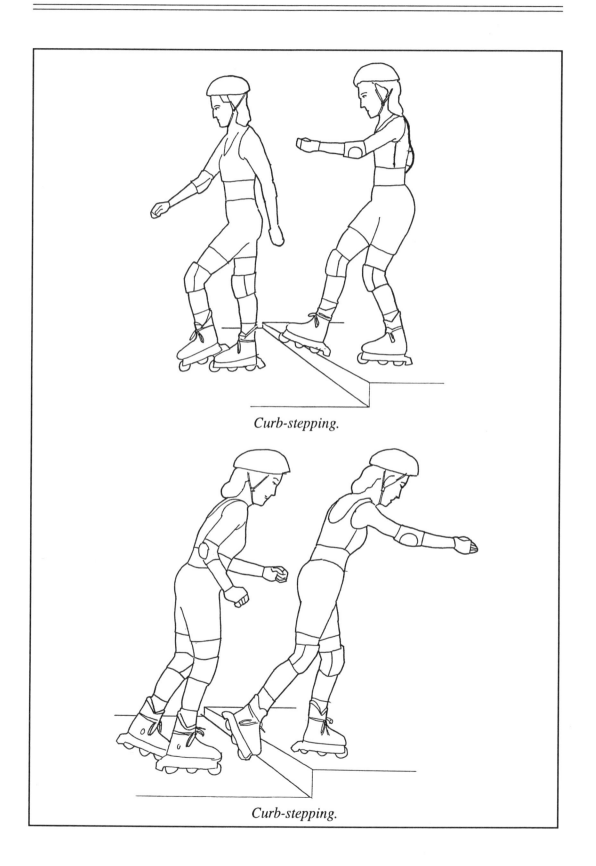

Curb-stepping.

Curb-stepping.

EVERYONE'S RESPONSIBILITY

As more and more aspiring in-line skaters and conventional skate converts make their first tentative glides, does it not behoove us all — from skating product retailers to expert speed skaters — to stress the importance of safety, courtesy towards others, and respect for the device itself?

WHO WILL TEACH THE CHILDREN?

Unfortunately for the immediate and future growth of the in-line skating community, there are a handful of retailers, mail order houses, and shoddy manufacturers whose only care is to keep their cash registers ringing. This presents a significant problem. Let me illustrate.

John P. Beginner humbly walks into a sporting goods store, looking to buy his first pair of in-line skates. He knows nothing about them, except that everyone calls them Rollerblades® for some reason. He spots a red-vested Mae I. Helpue and asks for some assistance with the in-line skates. Mae, not knowing any better, points Johnny to a pallet of boxed Scream Machine in-line skates. Johnny finds his size and pays the cashier $19.95 and tax. Johnny, brimming with glee, straps on his Screamers, stands up, and leans way back, losing his balance. His feet, in full-throttle reverse, keep rolling but Johnny keeps falling back. KA-BOOM! Johnny lands backside on a parking pylon. With a sore rump and utter contempt for in-line skating, Johnny goes home and plays Nintendo®.

Consider, if you please, what has occurred here.

The heel brake. The most basic braking technique and the only "built-in" braking device.

Essentially, there are three methods by which a customer can purchase a pair of in-line skates. Tom Peters, of *In Search of Excellence* fame, would call this "point of entry." Simply stated, this refers to the point at which a potential customer comes into contact with the greater retail market. To simplify further, I will refer to these "points" as primary, secondary, and tertiary sellers.

The primary seller is an exclusive retailer of in-line skates and related equipment. These proprietors typically offer a package of complimentary training with your purchase. A free "test roll" to help with your decision is also common. You are treated as a potential member of a greater community, not a mere line item on a ledger sheet.

Next there are the secondary sellers. These retailers are the smaller sporting goods stores that specialize in a handful of sporting activities. You may find salespeople who are knowledge-able about in-line skating because they skate themselves. Although they may offer some guidance in making a selection, "sport mart" clerks cannot give you the basic instruction to "hit" the road without landing on it!

Finally, there are tertiary retailers. Department stores, shoe marts, home shopping channels, hyper marts, mail order, and (ugh!) convenience stores. The core problem is that no one spe-cializes in anything. Big-store clerks are the consummate "know-it-alls" who know nothing! Indeed, you would be lucky to find your shoe size, never mind the only "omni-clerk," who is doubtless preoccupied with midday stocking.

So, fellow skater, my point is this. Show me a responsible retailer who is knowledgeable about and enamored with the in-line skating product and activity, and I will show you safer streets and a peaceful coexistence with the community.

8.
In-Line Skating
Techniques

● ●

If there is any sport you cannot properly learn by reading a book, it is in-line skating. What follows is intended to serve as an *introduction* to some of the techniques used in in-line skating. No writer of an instruction manual can anticipate every personality, every question, every hang-up a beginning skater may encounter. Suffice it to say that this portion of the book is intended to be used as a reference to familiarize yourself with basic techniques, the terminology, and a conceptual knowledge of in-line skating. It is not intended to replace a qualified instructor.

I have included enough information in this volume for you to locate someone who can offer you the much needed personal attention and feedback that I am unable to give each reader through a book.

BALANCE AND POSTURE

A balanced center of gravity is the foundation of a good in-line skating technique. Keep your knees bent, ankles flexed forward, and body balanced over the balls of your feet. Your back should be straight, stomach in, shoulders even, head up, and eyes forward. Don't stare at your skates. As your speed increases, your world will begin to flash by like so many flickering images seen while looking through a train window. Keep your eyes moving.

STOPPING/BRAKING

There are several ways to stop yourself. It is vital that before you learn to GO, you first be able to STOP. The heel brake is typically the first method you learn in order to stop. The key to it is balanced leverage.

The Heel Brake
TECHNIQUE

Lean slightly toward your left skate and extend your right (braking) foot forward, creating a scissors effect. Your toe should be up, brake pad down. (If you are left-handed, you will probably want to reverse these instructions.)

Once extended, push the right heel into the pavement while maintaining a flat, even-pressured stance on the left foot.

Lean forward into your stop, while bending your left knee fully and your right knee slightly. Both legs are brought together at the knees, arms extended for balance.

In-line skating instructor Ken Moody teaching the basics to a beginner taking her first tentative glides. Courtesy of Crunch, New York City.

A perfect first attempt at a heel brake. Notice that her feet are properly "scissored," her weight is balanced, her hands are forward, and she is in control.

The "pigeon-toed" stance. This is the best way to stand when you don't want to roll; it is essential when you are on an unlevel surface.

SUMMARY

Just as a new pair of shoes remains a bit stiff until worked in, so does a heel brake until it has been worn down by use. If you find that you cannot create braking leverage quickly, in-line and in control, have your local skate shop grind the brake down a little.

TIP

If you have trouble maintaining balance, put your hands on your knees as you apply the foot brake.

The T-Stop

OBJECTIVE

The T-Stop is more popular among advanced skaters. While the appeal is largely aesthetic, it is a very effective way to moderate your speed. Ultimately, the more stopping options you have, the more likely it is for you to avoid skating hazards.

The T-stop requires you to drag one skate perpendicular to your forward line of movement. Because you are using the friction between the edge of your wheels and the surface, the wear on your wheels may drive you to the automated cash machine more than you would like, but it is the cost of doing business![24]

TECHNIQUE

While rolling forward, scissor your skates so that your right support leg (or left, whichever is more comfortable) is leading your left leg. Lift your left skate a few inches off the ground, turning the toe outward. Place your left toe down, to the side, and behind you while keeping your weight on your support leg.

With both knees bent, drag your left skate in toward the heel of your right foot. Gradually shift your weight to the back skate on the inner edge of your wheels. As you apply pressure on the edge of your wheels, the back skate will probably pull away, especially on a coarse surface. Flex the ankle farther and gradually add weight onto your right heel. Continue dragging, pressing downward until you come under control.

TIP

Before you become too fond of this braking technique, note that you will quickly wear through a lot of wheels (and money) unless you alternate with other stopping techniques. Furthermore, the T-stop is not always effective for high speeds or steep hills because of your body's uneven balance.

The Power Stop

OBJECTIVE

The Power Stop is an advanced form of braking. Although this braking technique originated in ice hockey, it is regularly utilized in in-line skating as an effective and quick method of slowing down.

TECHNIQUE

Begin by rolling forward with both legs parallel and your knees slightly bent. Next, put as much weight as you can on your right skate and scissor it slightly forward. Lift your left foot, allowing wheels #1 and #2 to "catch" on the pavement. Pivot that skate one-half turn so that it is facing to the rear — in the opposite direction that you are skating. At this point, your weight should be evenly distributed.

Finally, extend your right leg so that your wheels are perpendicular both to the road and your left (rear) skate. Extend your right leg and place your right skate at an angle, shallow enough

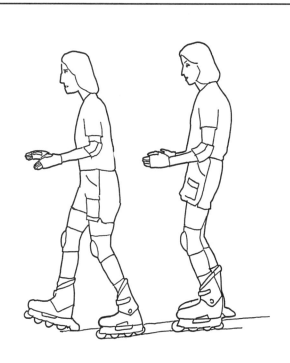

The heel brake.

The T-stop.

Halfway there! During races, resting one or both arms on the small of the back can conserve energy and improve aerodynamics. Notice that her elbow is properly tucked close to her body.

so that the inner edge of your wheels slides along the ground. (Imagine shaving a layer of ice with your skate, easy to do if you have been ice skating!) As you begin your slide, transfer some weight from your left foot to your right to place more pressure between your sliding wheels and the ground.[25]

SUMMARY

This is the most physically demanding of the braking techniques. Your legs and groin must be very limber so that you can pivot your trailing skate a complete 180 degrees (i.e., stretch!). It also helps if you have slightly worn wheels, as they will slide more easily along "grippy" asphalt. In fact, while learning, it is well advised that you find a very smooth area of *concrete*, not asphalt. With concentrated practice, and doubtless a couple sets of wheels, you will be well on your way to stopping on a dime!

A final caveat. To initiate an effective slide across the skating surface, you must have a shallow enough angle and sufficient speed to overcome the wheels' innate tendency to stick to the surface. Otherwise your wheels *will* stick, and like the brakes locking on a motorcycle, you will be hurled headlong over your "sliding" foot, which did not do much sliding at all! If you are lucky, you will land on the seat of your pants.

Two critical points to remember: Bend your back leg, and when angling the inner edge of your skate wheels to the ground, *almost* place your inner angle on the pavement. This will create the extreme angle that you need to achieve to stop.

"SCULLING"
Objective

"Sculling"[26] is a great way to get acclimated to in-lining. You get the feel of moving forward without committing to a full stride.

TECHNIQUE

Begin upright with your knees slightly bent. Toes should be at a 45-degree angle facing out. Using the inside edge of your wheels, let both skates glide evenly until your feet are just beyond your shoulder line. Using your momentum, pivot on your heels and point your toes and knees inward. Simultaneously begin to pull your feet together until they are back to their original position.

Continue this movement until it is fluid and continuous, and you are able to control your width and speed. Remember to bend your knees and push with an outward motion, followed by straightening and squeezing inward.[27]

TIP

If you have trouble getting your initial momentum, try taking a few choppy steps. Then settle into your sculling movement.[28]

BASIC STRIDE
Objective

You are now ready to start incorporating your whole body into in-line skating. In-line skating is the only sport I know of where gravity actually works for you. Because striding is fundamentally a "side-to-side" movement, gravity naturally pulls your skates to the side.

Technique

Bend your knees and waist, point your feet outward at a 45-degree angle, and push your right foot directly to the side with the inside edge of your wheels. Shift your weight to the left foot as you push off with your right. Lean forward into the direction you are headed.

At the end of your push-off, while keeping your weight on your left leg, lift up your free right foot and return to a standing parallel roll. Next, try pushing your left foot directly to the side and balancing on your right foot. Return to a standing parallel roll.[29]

Continue balancing on one leg as you push off with the other, always returning your feet to a standing parallel roll.

TIP

If you have trouble with your initial push-off, bend at the waist and place your hands on your knees.

MAXIMIZING YOUR STRIDE

If you have ever played tennis or golf, you know that maximizing your swing starts with a back swing. The logic is this — the longer the swing, the greater amount of force is generated. The same principle applies to striding. To get the most from your stride, bring your feet together following each push-off. When you bring your feet together and begin your stride from the center position, you maximize your energy output, thus achieving the greatest distance out of each stride.

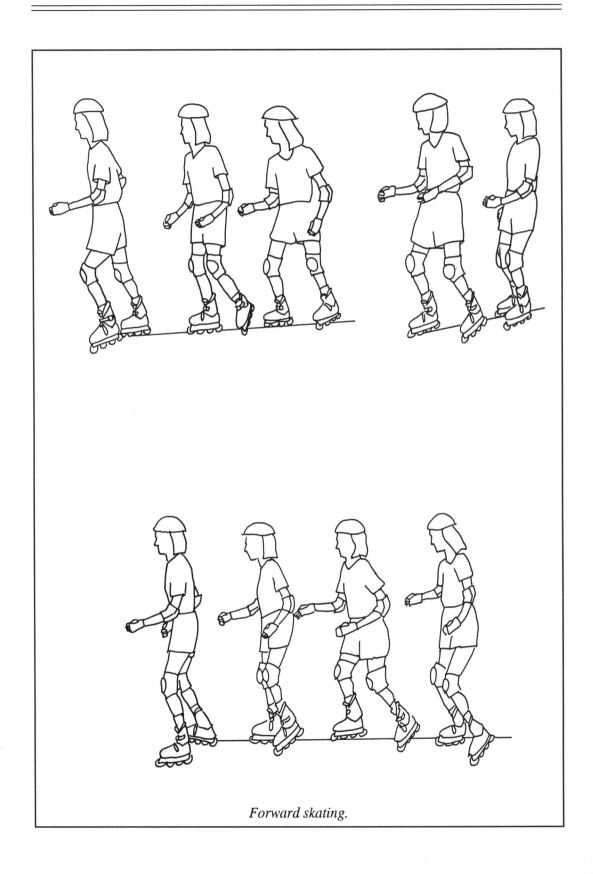

Forward skating.

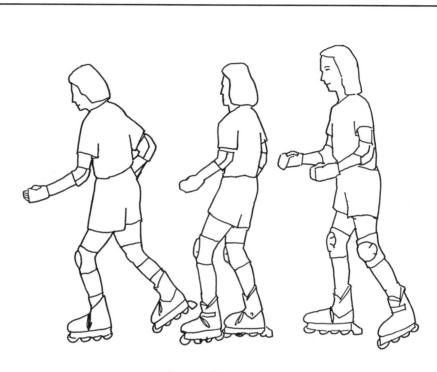

Forward skating.

Rock 'n roll.

MOVING FORWARD
Objective

The easiest way to begin forward in-line skating is to *rock 'n roll.*

Technique

The technique is simple. Begin with your feet parallel and your knees comfortably bent. With a side-to-side (lateral) movement, start by leaning from your left skate to your right. Continue to shift your weight and position your toes so that they are turned out at approximately a 45-degree angle. Continue rocking from left to right and lean forward. If you are rolling at a snail's pace, try turning your toes farther out and trust yourself.

Once you have started to roll, try stopping with the heel brake that you learned earlier. The key benefit to mastering the rock 'n roll is to feel comfortable with the skates moving under you. At first, it may seem uncomfortable or unstable. (Do you remember what learning to ride a bicycle was like?) Just remember to keep your knees bent and *never* lean or "sit" back. This is one of the "sins" of in-line skating.

TURNS
Basic

OBJECTIVE

Choose a skating area free of obstacles. Parking lots and vacant playgrounds are ideal.

TECHNIQUE

To turn, begin by shifting your weight so that you are on the edge of your wheels. The more weight you are able to place on the edge of your skate, the more responsive and sharper your turn will be.

To turn left, first visualize turning left. Place your weight on the inside edge of your right foot. Bend the knees to increase the angle and force on the edge. Complete the turn by moving your head, hands, and knees in the direction you wish to turn. Maintain your bend in the knees. That's it. It's really quite simple!

TIP

When starting out, keep your movement simple. In-line skates are very responsive. Take a deep breath, relax, and visualize a smooth and fluid turn — you will do fine.

Crossover Turn

OBJECTIVE

The crossover turn is a more advanced, more efficient turn that allows you to maintain and increase your speed as you change directions. Again, find a flat wide open area in which to practice.

TECHNIQUE

Begin with your stronger side. You will know your stronger side from the beginning. Everyone has a strong and a weak side, just as you have a writing hand or a throwing arm.

Start by stepping the right foot over the left (or vice versa), and the left over the right. Continue to repeat this movement until you are comfortable with it. Maintain your balance on the right skate and swing the left skate out, across, and down so that your legs are crossed at the thigh and your feet are parallel (both outer sides of your skates should be facing each other). Hold that position and maintain your balance. Then return your left skate to the original parallel

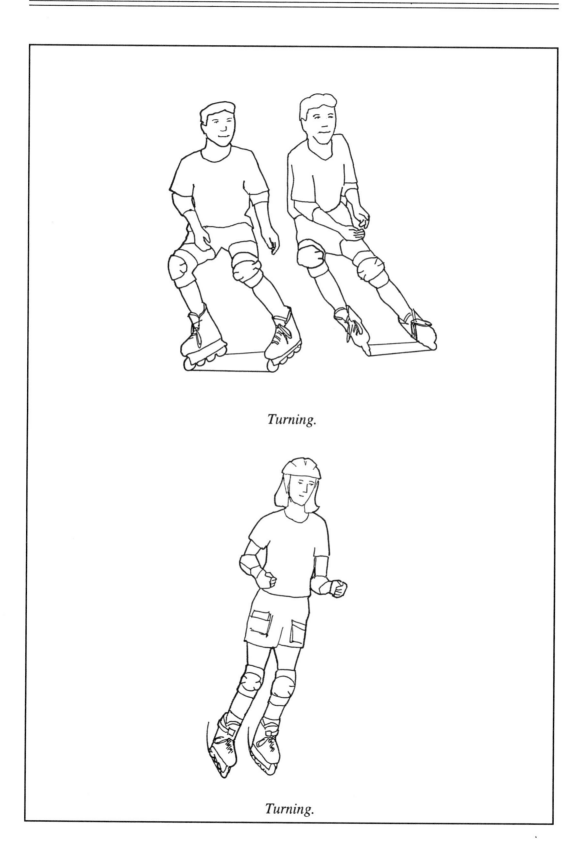

Turning.

Turning.

Take a good look at Eddy Matzger's body position. Training at the autodromo in Mexico City, Matzger is a master of the sport and among the finest skaters anywhere. Courtesy of Team Karim.

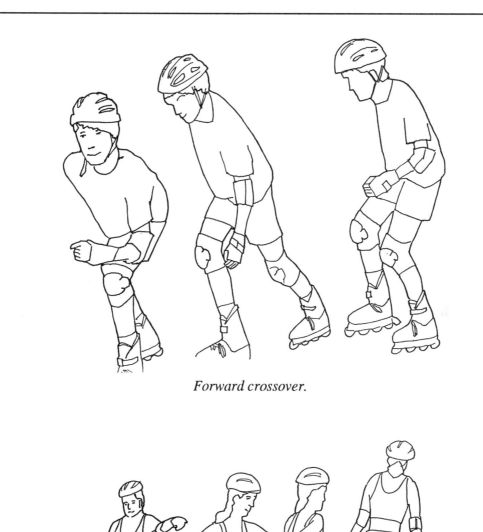

Forward crossover.

Forward crossover.

Backward skating.

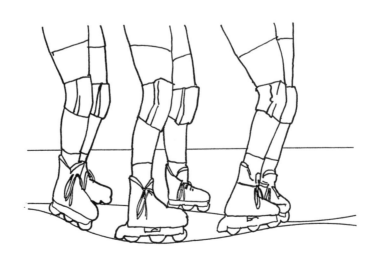

Backward skating.

position (both inner sides of your skates are facing each other). Repeat this exercise until you are comfortable with it and can maintain your balance each time.

Now imagine walking sideways to the right. The left skate goes up, crosses the right skate, and goes back to the ground; right skate up, crosses the left skate, and back to the ground; and so on. It is vitally important that you be on a flat surface. Otherwise, with each step you will be progressively rolling downhill. Repeat again and again.

Next, add a bit of a roll to the crossover step. Imagine a fusion of the crossover and the stride. Start by pushing yourself into an easy forward roll. Your weight is being transferred from left to right. Don't actually stride or you will go too fast.

As you push off with the right skate, shift your weight to the left foot. Keeping your leg bent, lift your right skate, point the toe, and slowly cross it over your left leg and down to the ground. Both skates must be parallel, or each skate will go in its own direction.

Upon contact with the ground, shift your weight to your right foot, and lift and recover your left foot to a parallel roll.[30]

TIP

To avoid getting your skates entangled during the crossover, make sure that the toe of your skate is pointed in the direction of your turn. The sharpness and degree of the turn are determined by your body position. If you go into a turn relatively upright, your turn will not be as extreme as if you bend your knees and lean into the turn. A good way to practice turning is to create a large imaginary circle on the ground and practice going around it several times in one direction. Reverse your direction, and work on turning in the other direction. As you feel more comfortable, you can begin to spiral in toward the center of the circle to tighten your turns. The ability to make sharp, hairpin turns is a valuable technique in avoiding obstacles.

BACKWARD STOPPING/BRAKING
Objective

Before you attempt to skate backward, you must learn how to stop backward! Considering that your heel brake is on the back of your skate, it's reasonable, if not entirely obvious, to conclude that it cannot be used while skating backward. If you are stubborn enough to discover this for yourself, you will not only fall hard on the seat of your pants, you will likely mangle your arms and wrists due to your innate tendency to break a fall.

The best way to stop while skating backward is to turn around and face forward. Logically, once you are facing forward, you can use the heel brake (or any other braking method you desire) to stop yourself.

Technique

Stand with your legs parallel. Look over your shoulder, either right or left — whichever is more comfortable. Pivot your right (or left) leg 180 degrees so that your right leg is facing away from you. Bring your left (or right) leg around to meet with your right. You are now rolling forward and can stop using your heel brake.

Once you have the ability to stop backwards or any other direction, your enjoyment will increase in tune to your confidence level. Ultimately, *you* have to say when to go and when to stop. See to it that you can.

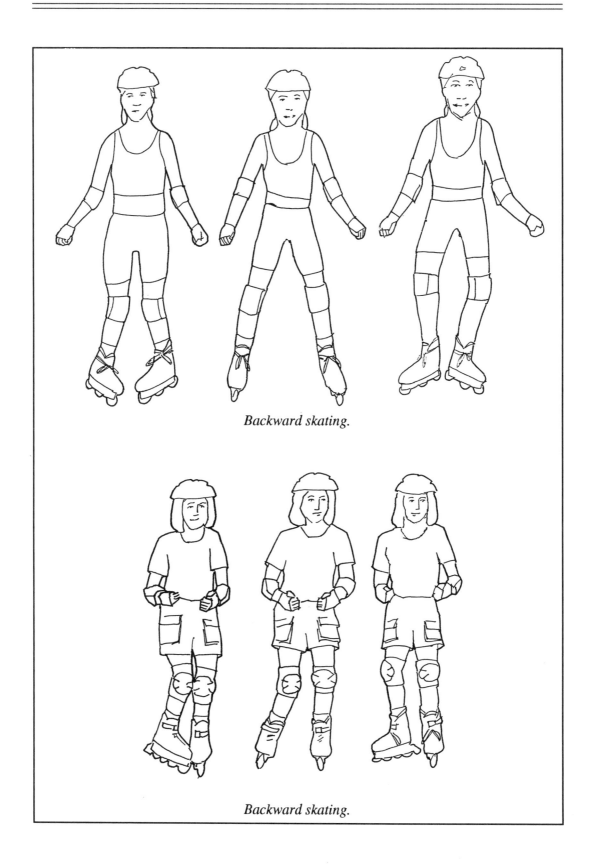

Backward skating.

Backward skating.

Ron Lowrie, Eddy Matzger, Doug Glass (left to right) at the Phoenix Rollerblade Series '91. Courtesy of Team Karim.

BACKWARD "SCULLING"
Objective

Skating backward often stirs a bit of anxiety in the beginning in-line skater. This is natural. We like to see where we are going. The best way to conquer your anxiety is through visualization and being confident.

Technique

To scull backward, you use the same movements you learned in forward sculling with a few modifications. Instead of pushing off with your heels, you end your stroke with the accent on your toes.

Begin with your feet and knees turned inward at a 45-degree angle. Using the inner edge of your wheels, lean forward. You will feel as though you are falling. "Relax and let your skates glide out evenly to the side beyond your shoulder line. Keep your weight forward."[31]

TIPS

As you improve skating backward, you can learn to stroke one leg at a time and do crossover strokes while turning.

If you are not moving, try increasing the angle of your feet (pigeon-toed).

BACKWARD STRIDE
Objective

Backward and forward striding are very similar. The primary difference is that in backward striding, you begin with your foot flat on the ground and finish the stride with your toe.

Technique

Begin with your legs at shoulder width. Shift your weight from one foot to the other. When you are ready to roll backward, point your toes in, lean forward, and continue rocking side to side. "If your weight is forward and your toes are pointed inward, you should be rolling" backward at this point.[32] If you feel that you are leaning too far forward and you are going to fall, ease back a bit but don't lean back. Try bending more at the knees. Start with a two-legged backward scull and begin your in-out-in-out technique.

Begin a one-legged scull by adding some extra weight on the inner edge of your right skate. Return the right skate to a parallel position to prepare for the scull with the left foot. Alternate your scull from one skate to another, ultimately returning to the parallel position before you begin your next move.

ADVANCED TECHNIQUES
Racing Theory

Throughout all sports, speed has been the athlete's aphrodisiac. Although in-line skating will doubtless see more and more innovations in the next several years (indeed, it already has — Roller Tennis, RollerBungy jumping, sail skating, etc.), racing through the wind will remain the sport's mainstay.

Stroke and Glide

OBJECTIVE

Unless you are sprinting, the key is to maximize every stride by making long, fluid, powerful strokes.

TECHNIQUE

To cut through the wind with minimum resistance and to maintain your forward momentum, bend your knees and waist. Your knees should be bent at approximately a 90 degree angle. To maximize each stroke, make sure you return your legs directly under your body to the point where your knees almost make contact. This is of vital importance, as the most powerful acceleration is generated from the initial eighteen inches of your stride. Nevertheless, finish your stroke completely to maximize your rhythm.

Again, skating enables you to utilize gravity. As you begin to push out your skate, gravity's forces work with the power you exert. Thus, motion of your stroke is a side-to-side motion, not a front-to-back technique. If you think about it logically, with a front-to-back motion, your skates would simply roll back and forth and take you nowhere, as though you were running up a down escalator.

To maximize your efficiency during the stroke and glide, it is important to keep your upper body movement to a minimum. This is best achieved by leaning and bending in the direction you are skating and putting one or both hands behind you. This will help you form a natural tuck position. Pumping your arms during the bulk of the race does not help much, as it creates resistance, dissipates your forward glide, and consumes energy. Save your arm swing for mid-race and final sprints to the finish line.

Drafting

Recall, if you will, your last long distance road trip on the interstate. Did you notice eighteen-wheel trucks forming a mini-convoy in which one truck was tucked in back of another?

In speed skating, this technique is called drafting. The reason for drafting is that the forward-most skater cuts through the wind, creating an air pocket immediately behind him. If you can skate in that air pocket, you will be at a great advantage, since you will no longer be fighting wind resistance.

Generally, most drafting occurs in races in 10K and up. During the bulk of the race, skaters work in packs to conserve energy for when they need it most — the final sprint.

Hills

OBJECTIVE

Skating uphill requires strength and endurance. The hill's grade, gravity, force, and the effort you put into the workout will determine both the level of difficulty and ultimately what you get out of it. Nevertheless, for a great workout, there are few more challenging.

TECHNIQUE

Essentially, there are two methods of ascending a hill: striding and chopping. The method you choose, like the hill you choose, depends on the hill's grade and your fitness level.

Striding uphill requires several adjustments from striding on a level surface. First, lowering your body will increase the length of your stride. As you increase your speed, gradually bring your torso up, increasing the angle of the upper body from the waist. Experiment with the angle of your body to see what works best for you.

Chopping looks a bit strange, but you should know what it is and how to do it. Begin by running (literally) uphill with the toes of your skates pointed out. Your steps should be short and choppy. The steeper the hill, the shorter and choppier they become. This technique tends to expend energy quickly, so you may want to vary your hill climbing technique between chopping and striding.

TIP

If you need to rest before you get to the top of the hill, be sure that your skate position forms a "V" (while facing into the hill) so that you do not roll backwards.

Racing Disclaimer

The following is a sample of a race disclaimer. If you race or plan on competing, take a look at what you are agreeing to.

I know that skating a road race is a potentially hazardous activity. I should not enter and skate unless I am medically able and properly trained. I also know that, although police protection will be provided, there may be traffic on the course route. I assume the risk of skating in traffic. I also assume all other risks associated with skating this event, including but not limited to falls, contact with other participants, the effects of weather, including heat and/or humidity, and the conditions of the roads, all such risks being known and appreciated by me. Knowing these facts, and in consideration of your acceptance of my entry fee, I hereby for myself, my heirs, executors, administrators, or anyone else who might claim on my behalf, covenant not to sue, and waive, release, and discharge COMPANY ABC and ORGANIZATION XYZ and any other organization associated with the race, and the local government and the police, volunteers and any and all sponsors, including their agents, employees, assigns, or anyone acting for/on their behalf from any and all claims or liability for death, personal injury, or property damage of any kind or nature whatsoever arising out of, or in the course of, my participation, even though that liability may arise out of negligence or carelessness on the part of the persons and entity named above or even if such persons and entity are otherwise strictly liable. This release and waiver extends to all claims of every kind and nature whatsoever, foreseen or unforeseen, known or unknown. The undersigned further grants full permission to COMPANY ABC and any other sponsor of this race and any organization conducting the race and/or agents authorized by them, to use any photographs, videotapes, motion pictures, recordings, or any other record of this event for any purpose.

I have read the foregoing and certify my agreement by my signature.

If under eighteen years of age, signature of parent or guardian is required.

9.
Injuries and Discomfort

FALLS

You will fall. Everyone does. The most common contact areas are the wrists, shoulders, tailbone, elbows, knees, and head. It makes sense. All those areas of your body "stick out" in one way or another. So it should be no wonder that the protective gear for in-line skating is designed for those vulnerable areas. This is the key point: If you wear your protective gear, you will avoid avoidable injuries.

The proper way to fall when skating is head-first. (Note: This does not mean *on* your head.) It will be difficult at first, but you should be wearing equipment designed just for this purpose.

Because everyone with a sense of balance carries some sensory "baggage" about falling, you need to practice, on either soft dirt or a grass field.

The best thing you can do to become a great "faller" is *relax*. Tense muscles tear. The next best thing you can do is lower your center of gravity. By doing so, you lessen the distance you have to fall; thus, your body will absorb less shock. To lower your center of gravity, bend your waist and try to put your hands on your knees.

Now for the fall. When you do fall, guide your impact toward your protected areas — wrists, elbows, knees, in that order. *Stay relaxed.*

If you are traveling at high speeds, you will have to deal with inertia — the tendency to keep moving. The key again is to *relax* and roll (if you must) until you have dissipated your momentum.

Get up, dust yourself off, and do it 500 more times. (Just kidding!) Take a break and GET IN-LINE!

CUTS AND ABRASIONS

These are road burns from falling. You will not die from a road burn, but it is very important to avoid infection by washing the wound with soap and water as soon as possible. Make sure you keep the wound covered with a clean bandage. Bandannas make great multi-purpose bandages.

KNEES

Treat your knees like jewels. They are so valuable to you, but they were not designed very well. They absorb most of the impact of your body, and allow you to twist and turn when skating. Always be aware of internal "knee alert" — pain under the kneecap, "clicking/creaking sounds" when bending, etc.

Keep your knees warm, protected, and flexible through stretching. Whenever you feel pain, pull over and take a look.

BLISTERS

We all dread this accumulation of water under the skin. Blisters are created by two elements — heat and friction. The skin reacts by cooling the overheated area with a pocket of water that ultimately creates more pain for us. The best way to cope with blisters is never to get them.

If, despite your efforts, you still get a blister, treat it properly and you will minimize further pain and a possible infection.

Use an ice pack, whether at home or on the road, to numb the area of the blister. This will help to alleviate the pain. To drain the blister, sterilize a sewing needle (or use a syringe) with a match flame and then swab the blister with rubbing alcohol. Puncture it in several places and gently push the fluid out from all sides until it appears to be fairly well drained. Leave the skin of the blister intact. Do not try to remove it since this will expose raw and as yet unprotected skin underneath the blister "roof."

For blisters on the bottom of the feet, use a round piece of moleskin with an inner circle cut out to expose the blister. Place the moleskin over the blister so that the blister is exposed in the center, but is protected by the surrounding moleskin. For a toe blister, the same procedure should be followed with the addition of applying sterile gauze. This prevents the toe blister from nudging the toe box of your shoes. A blister should receive a light application of iodine to prevent infection. Note: Some expert and professional in-line skaters advocate leaving the blister intact and untouched. Eddy Matzger, for example, leaves blisters intact and finds that a callus forms well without draining the blister.

CALLUSES

A callus is an accumulation of thick, dead skin. This is your body's attempt to protect the skin from irritation. Calluses serve a practical function, so do not treat them unless they give you problems.

If they do, try using medicated pads, pumice stones, lotions with urea, or soaking in warm water. As the calluses begin to wear and skin spurs develop, use a pair of cuticle scissors or a toenail cutter to remove.

FOREIGN BODIES

What is a foreign body? Anything that gets stuck under your skin and does not belong there. The most common objects are pebbles, splinters, and glass.

If you cannot remove the object yourself, or if it begins to swell and redden, see a physician as soon as possible.

Although various home treatment procedures exist, I will not endorse one here. Removing a foreign object from underneath your skin is a form of surgery. I urge you to consult the advice of a doctor before attempting to remove any foreign object from underneath the skin by yourself.

INGROWN TOENAILS

If you do not already own a pair, buy some toenail clippers. Ingrown toenails are usually caused by neglect. If a remedy is needed, gently lift the edge of the nail with a cuticle stick or your fingernail and place a piece of cotton under the skin. Avoid liquid remedies that shrink the skin. In a few days, you should be able to trim the nail with scissors or clippers. Inspect toenails daily and keep them trimmed.

10.
Types of In-Line Skating

RECREATIONAL

With perhaps the exception of athletes seeking the cross-training benefits of in-line skating, most of the newly initiated in-line skaters fall into the generic "recreational" category. Indeed, millions — and the projected tens of millions soon to venture into in-line skating — skate for the fun and love of it. Young or old, in-line skating will bring you years of fun for hours at a time. It is one of few individual sports that is inherently social.

FITNESS

In-line skating is an outstanding form of exercise. An hour on skates consumes nearly the same amount of calories as an hour of running or cycling, without the pavement pounding that running exerts upon your body. Indeed, in-line skating, arguably the leading low-impact activity next to cross-country skiing, relieves the concerns of the vitamin-popping fitness fanatic.

Evidence released in a 1990 study at St. Cloud State University found that forty-five minutes of in-line skating three times a week over an eight-week period yielded a one-percent reduction in body fat. It further revealed a twenty-percent increase in aerobic fitness, improved muscular capacity in the hips and knees, with a simultaneously decreasing waist size by roughly one inch. Not least of all, these results were achieved without the pounding skeletal stress incurred while running or doing high-impact aerobics.

Aerobic versus Anaerobic Training

Our bodies have two ways to create energy. One method is with oxygen (aerobic), and the other creates energy in the absence of oxygen (anaerobic). Anaerobic exercise uses oxygen for small periods of time, usually just a few minutes. Running the 100-yard dash or bench pressing 150 pounds is an anaerobic activity. Anaerobic activities use a small burst of energy. Lifting weights and using Nautilus or Cybex equipment at the gym, as I once did, is not useless. Adequate body strength complements overall fitness.

Aerobic exercise produces ninety percent of the body's needed oxygen, both in exercise and at rest. "Aerobics," as it is now called, is a series of exercises that requires a maximum amount of oxygen.

The problem with getting fit for fitness' sake is that there are many ways to do it, but so often we become bored with trying to feel good about ourselves. Imagine eating food that had no flavor but was simply for nourishment value. Being a fairly clever animal, we added some zing and spice to our food. And now we love to eat! In simple language, complete fitness requires that you increase your body's endurance by increasing and sustaining your breathing rate for a period of at least twenty minutes. This is called *aerobic* fitness. By increasing and sustaining the heart rate during exercise, you maximize your *oxygen transport ability*. Recall the last time you walked up a long flight of stairs. Your breathing may have begun to increase because your muscles were not getting enough fuel (oxygen) quickly enough.

When your body "runs out" of oxygen or it is no longer able to meet its need, the muscles are able to go on working for a period of time. This is known as *anaerobic* fitness. When we begin an exercise routine, many of us feel a bit sluggish. This is known as oxygen debt, and continues until we "warm up," increase our heart rate, and transport oxygen (fuel) to the bereft areas of our body.

In July 1992, the American Heart Association declared that lack of exercise is a major risk factor for heart disease, ranking it with the harmful effects of smoking, high cholesterol, and high blood pressure. Although the Association has long contended that physical inactivity raises the risk of heart disease, new scientific data has upgraded *lack of exercise* as a major risk in and of itself.

The good news is that sustained aerobic exercise twenty minutes a day, three to four times a week, is the best offense against lowering that risk substantially. Better still, in-line skating offers the ideal aerobic workout for competitors and lethargic fitness slugs alike. Moreover, in-lining suspends the stress and tedium of a typical day in a way few activities can — rejuvenating the body and mind through the rhythm it affords.

CROSS-TRAINING
Skating

You may recall from the section on the history of skating that cross-training was the catalyst for the creation of skating on wheels. More and more athletes from an ever-widening array of sports are discovering the benefits of in-line skating. It is quickly becoming a preferred method for off-season strength training.

For obvious reasons, the closest cousins of in-line skating — ice skating, performance skating, figure skating, and hockey — find in-line skating to be complementary. Perhaps the singular constant on which skaters of each type would agree is that their legs get very little rest. Moreover, even on the "glide" — that is to say, when muscles are being exerted the least — a skater's muscles are in a constant state of exertion. Since the leg is always in a fixed position, anaerobic (muscle strengthening) energy is required to meet the demand.

Cycling

Although mile for mile cycling offers the benefit of more efficient aerobic conditioning, in-line cross-training places greater demands on the leg muscles. Not only is the cyclist "resting" his weight on the saddle, but the upstroke (non-propulsive part) of cycling is quite short. Unless the cyclist is really pumping up an incline, the legs are not working about half of the time. Moreover, if you recall the last time you rode a bike, only your quadriceps and calf muscles are being worked. Skating, however, requires a stable foot nearly all the time; thus, both the quadriceps and the hamstrings are being used.

Ride like the wind. Copyright 1992 and courtesy of Jamie Budge.

Sail skating at El Mirage, California. Copyright 1992 and courtesy of Jamie Budge.

Running

While running utilizes aerobic energy pathways almost exclusively, skating has a large anaerobic component. Breath for breath, runners consume nearly thirty percent more oxygen than in-line skaters do. Skating, however, is more anaerobic-intensive. To match the muscle exertion of in-line skating, one would have to complete innumerable dizzying laps at the track.

For the strictly weight conscious, here is "food for thought." Easy in-line striding burns about ten calories per minute. Consider that against running's twelve calories per minute. Flip a coin. If it's heads, go skate. Tails? GET IN-LINE!

IN-LINE AEROBICS

It seems all so logical. Take the most popular fitness activity of the 1980s (aerobics), stir in a generous amount of sweat, seventy or so reverberating decibels of pop, top it off with the hottest sport around (in-line skating), and what have you created? In-line aerobics. In addition to offering in-line's assortment of activities, in-line aerobics, such as those offered by Crunch studio in New York City, features the ultimate in fun and fitness.

SAIL SKATING

So what do you call this? It's a surf-kite. A sail board? A wheeled-wind surfer!

It is called WindSkating and has been called many things throughout its fifteen-year history, but there is no mistaking the sheer joy, the wind-in-your-face freedom that comes from "riding the wind," as Jamie Budge, inventor and owner of WindSkate® Inc., describes it.

Riding the Wind

The principle of WindSkating, or "skate sailing" as the sport is known generically, is similar to its water counterpart, wind surfing. By harnessing the wind with a lightweight handheld sail, the in-line skater propels himself by tacking (zigzagging) across the wind.

Under ideal wind and surface conditions — continuous 15-20 mph wind is best — and with a knack for filling your sail with wind, WindSkaters routinely attain speeds of 30 mph from a 15 mph current; speed demons claim to have reached unofficial speeds just above 50 mph. As Keith Sherrins of San Gabriel explains, "It's like this burst of energy you feel — quieting, soothing, serene — if you can imagine serene speed."

Although Jamie Budge confides that he was not the first to conceive of a skate sailing device, he was the first and, for now, only inventor to establish a corporation to formalize his creation. While combing through patent archives to determine what kinds of similar devices existed, Budge recalls, "I saw all these god-awful designs with pulleys, doodads, and little contraptions with straps and balls." In reflecting on his own design, "Whatever divine bit of inspiration it was, I had never patented anything before or since. I have never considered myself an inventor."

Skateboards, Wheelchairs, and Beyond

From its conception, the WindSkate® has been modified to harness the wind to myriad wheeled and non-wheeled vehicles. The earliest WindSkate® was used with a skateboard. Like a wind-surf board, the sail sits in a socket as the rider leans to and fro. However, by 1978 skateboarding had taken a major dive in popularity, as roller-skating came into vogue and precipitated the first handheld WindSkate®. For five years, WindSkating with roller skates was enormously popular. A 1,400 mile WindSkate® marathon between Seattle and San Diego followed, as did sponsorships and media coverage.

Meanwhile, until Rollerblade® launched its enormously successful marketing campaign in 1983, thereby creating a new market for Budge, WindSkates® were configured to reach as many people as possible: in-line, roller, and ice skates; snow skis and skateboards; wheelchairs and anything else that could roll or slide. For instance, Budge, the consummate salesman, sold his SkiSkate as the "ultimate in skiing mobility" and dubbed it *wind-assist skiing.*

El Mirage: A WindSkater's Paradise

El Mirage Dry Lake Bed is about a two-hour drive from Los Angeles and twenty miles west-northwest of Edwards Air Force Base. The now-dry lake bed, which annually "fills" with an inch or so of water, spans four square miles.

The only visible sign of life atop this sunbaked lake bed is haphazard dunes of yucca weed and sand scattered in clusters called pucker mounds. The surface varies from a silky, glass-like veneer to a cobblestone husk, teeming with fissures forming a huge, puzzle-like formation.

Setting Sail

On my first occasion to set sail at El Mirage, I found that holding the sail and maneuvering it required minimal effort. I used the standard handheld WindSkate® BladeSail. Made of aluminum and Dacron® sailcloth, the sail is easy to maneuver, weighing in at seven pounds. The padded apex rests against either the left or right shin or thigh, depending on your height, while the hands grasp the cross-bar or spars to position the sail.

Upwind turns require that you flip the sail overhead (the sail resembles a hang glider in this position), while downwind turns are made by shifting your sail angle. Unlike some of the other sail designs for skateboards, in which the sail's apex utilizes a ball and socket device, the BladeSail, made especially for the in-line skater, produces a feeling of oneness with the sail — no straps, lines, or rigging. It is just like holding an oversized kite.

There is no doubt that WindSkating is easy to learn. Even a slow learner like myself was WindSkating within ten minutes. I found a little instruction enormously welcome, although at the time I was so centered on positioning the sail, I did not even notice which way the wind was blowing. By the second or third time out, your skills are automatic. And that's when the fun begins.

WindSkate® Information

Barring natural calamity or world war, 1993 should prove to be the best to date for WindSkate®, Inc. Slated for the last two weeks in May is the First Annual WindSkate® Championships. To be televised by the SportsChannel, the event is to be held at the El Mirage Dry Lake Bed. Among the scheduled events are a WindSkate Regatta, Hundred Yard Dash, Slalom Course, Free Style, Wind Flights, and Wind Dance.

For more information and a schedule of free demonstrations, contact:

WindSkate®, Inc.
P.O. Box 3081
Santa Monica, CA 90403
(310) 453-4808

FREESTYLE

Because of the newness of in-line skating, there are no rules to freestyle skating. In fact, what one may call a "sidewinder," another might refer to as a "grapevine." The only rule in freestyle

Playing in-line hockey. Courtesy of Rollerblade®, Inc.

is that anything goes. Whether it is a 180, 360, or 720, it is all about fun and self-expression.

Here are a couple of maneuvers you can try:

Toe-Toe

While rolling forward with your feet parallel, raise your right heel so you come onto your right toe. Lean forward and add a little weight to your toe. Use your left leg to give you a boost. Maintain your balance and lift your left heel up, coming onto your left toe. *Voilà!*

Curb Jumping

Curb jumping can give you a big thrill with a minimal jump. Before attempting a jump, be familiar with the course (i.e., road obstacles, peak traffic times, pedestrians, etc.) or check out the area first.

Approach the curb with a lowered body position, bent knees, and hands out in front. As you approach the edge of the curb, scissor your skates so you don't land flat-footed. Relax.

IN-LINE HOCKEY

Although there are several existing leagues and organizations for competitive and professional play, until the formation of the National In-Line Hockey Association (NIHA) in January 1993, the most organization an amateur hockey game saw was a group of players slapping a ball or "roller" puck around neighborhood backstreets or empty parking lots. Those thousands of individuals and preexisting local teams are in for a treat that is just over the horizon.

The National In-Line Hockey Association promises to create a national and unified organization of hockey teams, all playing under one set of rules and standards. These leagues are to be strictly amateur and non-contact in nature.

Standards of Play

The rules and regulations of in-line hockey are destined to evolve from the IISA's current rule book, "Amateur In-Line Hockey Rules and Regulations."

THE RINK

The rink, or surface of play, will average 188 feet by 88 feet.

GOAL POSTS AND NETS

The prescribed size for outdoor goalie nets is 42 inches high by 68 inches wide. For indoor play, the dimensions are 48 inches high by 72 inches wide.

TEAM SIZE

Each team is composed of five players and one goalie.

EQUIPMENT

Stick: The stick should not exceed 62 inches in length measured from the heel to the end of the shaft nor more than 12 inches from the heel to the end of the blade.

Skates: Players must wear in-line skates. Brakes are optional. "Quad" skates are also allowed.

Protective Equipment:

1.   Head protection.

2.   Face protection.

3.   Knee and shin protection.

4.   Jockstrap with cup.

5. Mouthpiece.

6. Elbow pads.

Youth must also wear face protection (cage or face shield).

Ball/Puck: The ball should be a uniform color and contrast with the color of the rink. It should weigh approximately 5.5 ounces and have a circumference no greater than 9 inches.

MATCH TIME

The maximum prescribed game duration should not exceed one hour with halftime(s) between play.

For a current rule book, contact the IISA or NIHA.

11.
The Future

●●●

LOOKING BACK — THE GREAT SKATE DEBATE

San Francisco, Golden Gate Park, 1979.

The summer of 1979 saw outdoor roller-skating skyrocket. By the end of the summer, there were an estimated 15,000 to 20,000 skaters using Golden Gate Park on Sundays, when the park was closed to all motor vehicle traffic. There were more than thirty skate vendor trucks that rented skates along the park border. Each truck carried between 200 and 500 pairs of skates. They often rented all of them. Skaters were everywhere!

Neighboring communities noticed. Soon there were complaints. Skaters took over the territory, sometimes blocking driveways and even urinating on front lawns. And as the numbers increased, so did the injuries. Worse still, the San Francisco Ambulance Service was stretched to the limit, responding to a large number of skate-related injuries.

The Department of Parks and Recreation had a dilemma. What were they going to do with all these skaters? To further complicate matters, the media took notice, pitting the skaters and the disaffected communities against each other. The controversy became known as "The Great Skate Debate." Sentiment to ban all skating in Golden Gate Park was strong. After months of contentious discussion and meetings, the Department of Parks and Recreation designated four areas in the park as restricted from skating. The Conservatory of Flowers, the Music Concourse, Stow Lake, and Children's Playground were known the world over and bustled with tourists and natives alike. The ultimatum demanded attention: if skaters could not stay out of the restricted areas, the Department would recommend a total skating ban in the Park.

Peter Ashe, then Assistant Superintendent of Parks and Recreation, presented the idea of forming a "skate patrol," which would be responsible for keeping skaters out of the restricted areas. Each skate vendor truck was to assign two skaters for "roller patrol" detail. A total of sixty skaters were solicited or simply volunteered, and the first skate patrol was formed. In due course, the city passed an ordinance banning all "recreational equipment vendors" from operating in San Francisco. But the skaters stayed. And due to their tireless efforts and love of the sport, the volunteer members of the red and white clad Golden Gate Skate Patrol, skating — roller, board, and in-line alike — are here to stay.

This example demonstrates how the sport of in-line skating can thrive and prosper in every community, if the participants act responsibly and work together to change the local laws if they believe the laws are unfair. Good luck with in-line skating in your own community.

THE OLYMPICS

Competitive in-line skating is making a successful bid for universal respectability. In fact, an international rule change opened elite competition to the in-line skater as well as the traditional "quad" skater. The 1992 Summer Olympic Games in Barcelona was the first time a roller sport — roller hockey — was featured as an exhibition sport at the Olympics. Looking beyond, the 1996 Olympic Games in Atlanta, Georgia will likely feature legitimate in-line skating as an exhibition sport at the very least. For the latest developments, contact the Atlanta organizing committee.

Atlanta Olympic Organizing Committee
Suite 3450, One Atlantic Center
1201 West Peachtree Street
Atlanta, GA 30309
(404) 874-1996

Epilogue

● ●

One World, One Community

Dear Reader:

Given the novelty of the sport of in-line skating, I had the pleasure of meeting many wonderful people, many of whom I have acknowledged. I have written, faxed, spoken with, and interviewed hundreds of people throughout the U.S., as well as in Europe, Canada, and Mexico. And if there is truth in numbers, then my telephone and postage bills speak volumes to my veracity.

Before I go, I would like to share an experience I had with one of these wonderful people. It was the last day. I would pack this beast in a box and be gone with it. But I had overlooked something. I found a small advertisement for reflector pins in one of the many newsletters I had been sent. Reflector pins! Why I made the call I do not know, but I am so glad I did.

I phoned and spoke with this man for about thirty minutes about his product. Before parting, I mentioned that I had a wonderful ink print of an in-line skate. I told him that I wished I could have found a poem about in-line skating to complement it. At any rate, I thanked him again and hung up.

About an hour later, I received a call. It was he. "Hello, Steve? It's Stan O'Connor again." Stan exemplifies what I have said all along — in-line skating attracts the best of humanity. It is not a group, a cult, a fad, a movement.

When Stan O'Connor called back, he said he had written the poem I had wished for about in-line skating. Here it is ….

Get In-Line!

In eighteen hundred and sixty-five
A new skate patent had come alive.
Instead of four wheels laid out in a square
Line them all up, and they would slice air.

But rolling along was a couples affair;
They'd skate at the rink, and preferred to be square.

In nineteen hundred and eighty-five
Four students had started, a skate, to derive.
Summer street hockey had lost all its charm.
Trip on your shoelaces; fall on your arm.
They needed a surface as smooth as the ice,
Though a skating improvement just might suffice.

But roller skates came in a standardized pair;
All the skates in the world were fact'ry-built, square.

All this square-wheeling business was rough on the feet.
The students' old hockey team kept getting beat.
A more fluidic motion had topped their concerns.
What was needed were skates they could put through the turns.

Twists and turns were so sudden; they couldn't prepare,
And they'd *BANG* hit the dirt, cursing skates that were square.

One summer day, in a student's bright mind,
popped a perfectly logical skating design.
Better than four-square, this could work fine:
Take the wheels off the sides, then install them in line.
He made up a pair, which he strapped to his feet.
The next day at practice, he couldn't be beat.

No street hockey players came close to compare
With wheels laid in a line; theirs were laid in a square.

The students had won, they gave up a shout!
Next day the four of them all were decked out.
In skates that were lighter, and faster, and turned.
One by one by the other teams, lessons were learned
In gracefully losing to players so fine.
The first men on earth to wear wheels in a line.

The students were asked to make skates by the pair.
In a while, they really knew they had something there.
Many years have gone by, and a skate revolution.
Laying wheels in a line was the perfect solution.
Engendering health, wearing tights in the street,
We strengthen our bodies, with wings on our feet.

Roller skating will never again be unfair

So good-bye to those skate wheels laid out in a square.
GET IN-LINE.

©1992 Stan O'Connor

Stan O'Connor, a former transcriber for *The Today Show* on NBC, lives with his wife and four-year-old son. When he's not writing poems, he makes SEE MEE fluorescent buttons to increase in-liners' visibility at night.

Glossary

● ●

ABEC — An acronym for the Annular Bearing Engineering Council. The bearings themselves are rated on a scale of one to nine with the acronym ABEC- placed in front of the number. Bearings rated by the Council are referred to as *precision bearings*, while bearings not rated by the ABEC receive the designation of *semi-precision* or *unground precision.*

AEROBIC — Means "with air." Refers to life forms that require oxygen. Also used to define specific types of exercise that use large amounts of oxygen.

AERODYNAMICS — The force of air upon an object.

AIR — As in catching or getting air. Used when achieving height from jumping (either from the ground, a ramp, or a pipe). Other air terminology is backward air, 180-degree air (turning while airborne), and airwalk (when you make a big scissors with your legs).

ALLEN WRENCH — A tool named after Joseph P. Allen. Used in the rotation of in-line skate wheels.

ANAEROBIC — The ability to live or grow without air or oxygen.

ANSI — Refers to the American National Standards Institute, which is based in New York and sets safety standards for protective equipment. ANSI's standards are regarded as easier to meet than those of Snell.

AXLE — A term that comes from figure skating. Refers to a one-half rotation in the air. There are also double and triple axles.

BAIL OUT — When you have lost control and need to stop very quickly. For instance, rolling onto a patch of grass after coming down a steep hill or avoiding a dangerous situation.

BAKE'N — When a skater is skating exceptionally well.

BEARING — An encasement containing seven ball bearings that are shielded and pre-packed in grease. Reduces friction and allows the wheel(s) to spin smoothly.

BLADING — Another term that refers to the sport of in-line skating.

BLOW-UP — Buckling or shattering of rigid pavement.

CANTERING — Moving the wheel frame of a skate toward the inside edge of the boot. This maximizes the length of the stride.

CENTER OF GRAVITY — The area of your body that is evenly balanced and distributed. This is the point on which the gravitational force acts. It is crucial to maintain your center of gravity to prevent falling.

CHANNELS/RUTS — Channelized depressions that develop in the tire tracks of asphalt and pavement. Frequently found in truck lanes on interstates due to the enormous weight of the trucks.

CONVENTIONAL SKATE — Refers to the original four-wheeled, rockering skate developed by James Plimpton. (See also QUAD SKATE.)

CORE — A central and fundamental part, located in the center portion of the wheel. Usually it is a nylon case that provides a hard case for the bearings to rest in. It locks to the wheel via slots molded into the wheel. A wheel's core may be its most important design element. Core shape, mass, and material can contribute to better stability, improved cornering, and the prevention of separation and blowout during normal use.

CROSS-TRAINING — Using one sport's conditioning benefits to improve performance in another sport.

CROSSOVER — An advanced turning technique, usually used by more advanced skaters traveling at greater speeds. The stride of the crossover turn requires the use of the inner edge of the right skate and the outer edge of the left skate.

DIAMETER — The size of the wheel. The diameter (a straight line passing through the center of the wheel) is measured in millimeters.

DOWEL BARS — Street bars embedded in pavement. They help to reduce possible faults.

DRAFTING — A racing technique that utilizes the low-pressure air current created when the wind is blocked by a racer in front of you.

DUCK WALK — Feet are skewed outward. The opposite of pigeon-toed.

DUROMETER — An instrument for measuring the hardness of polyurethane. The hardness of in-line wheels is measured on the "A" scale, which reflects increasing hardness. That is, 82a wheels are harder than 78a wheels. The current market range is about 74a to 93a. Softer wheels have greater traction, cornering, shock absorption, and rebound. Thus, they are better suited to rough surfaces and tight spaces. High durometer wheels should be used on smooth surfaces, by heavier people, and for longer wear life.

EDGE CRACKS — Cracks where pavement runs parallel to asphalt.

ELBOW/KNEE PADS — Protective/safety equipment with a reinforced plastic or foam-like shell to protect the arm and knee joints, which are most prone to injury and contact during a fall.

FREESTYLE — A general in-lining term for non-figure skating or racing movements.

GRASS RIDING — Skating on the grass.

HELMET — Protective head wear with inner shock-absorption and an outer protective shell. Perhaps the least often worn piece of safety equipment, and the most important.

HIGH-IMPACT — The combined force of gravity and body weight that exerts considerable stress throughout the legs and spinal column. Examples are running, field sports, and free-weight lifting.

HUB — The center component of the wheel, including the core, bearings, and spacers.

IISA — Acronym for the International In-Line Skating Association.

INDEPENDENT — A slalom maneuver in which you are in an extremely turned-out position and your legs are crisscrossing independent of each other.

INSOLES — The inner lining of footwear on which the foot rests.

JAMMIN' — Moving at a fast pace.

KICKIN' SOME ASPHALT — Skating.

LANE JOINT CRACKS — Separations along the seams between two paving lines.

LOW-IMPACT — The combined force of gravity and body that exerts relatively little stress on the skeletal structure. Examples are bicycling, swimming, and in-line skating.

LSD — Acronym for long slow distance. A method of endurance training.

MARATHON — Any long-distance or endurance race. Originally, a course of 26 miles, 385 yards run by a Greek runner between the cities of Marathon and Athens. Currently, the oldest and most well-known in-line marathon is the annual Athens to Atlanta (Georgia) Marathon, a course of eighty-five miles.

MERLIN, JOSEPH — The first inventor of the roller skate to receive a patent. Patented in 1863.

MOTORPACING — An endurance training technique utilizing a pace vehicle that guides the training athlete(s).

NIHA — National In-Line Hockey Association; founded in Miami, Florida in 1993. Sponsored by Rollerblade®, Inc. and IISA. Destined to be the most significant governing body in amateur in-line hockey.

OLSON, SCOTT — Inventor and developer of both the original Rollerblade® skate and the SwitchIt® Interchangeable Skate System. Current founder and president of O.S. Designs, Inc.

ORTHOTICS — Cushioned inserts scientifically designed to correct aberrations in the feet.

OXYGEN DEBT — The state when your body is not delivering oxygen to your extremities fast enough, resulting in a feeling of sluggishness.

OXYGEN-TRANSPORT CAPACITY — The amount of oxygen that each heartbeat delivers to the rest of the body.

PEEP — Clothing that is ripped or torn by a ramp or pavement.

PIGEON TOES — A very stable standing position in which the toes are pointed in and the heels are pointed out.

POLING — A form of in-line skating used while slaloming. Also used in cross-training to simulate the "plant and turn" of Nordic skiing and the arm motion of cross country skiing. Studies conclude that poling increases the heart rate and maximizes upper body conditioning.

POLYURETHANE — Technically speaking, any polymer that contains NHCO (nitrogen, hydrogen, carbon, oxygen) chemical linkages. In simpler language, this means smoother speed. This is the primary material used in the manufacture of in-line skate wheels.

POTHOLE — Ubiquitous, bowl-shaped holes of various sizes in pavement.

POWER SLIDE — A method of stopping using the edge of the wheels angled against the surface.

POWER STRAP — An additional buckle to tighten the cuff or the top skate boot.

PROFILE — The make-up of the rolling surface.

PROTECTIVE CUP — A padded plastic device used by men to protect the groin area. Protective cups are typically used in contact sports. Wear is strongly advised while playing roller hockey and street hockey.

PTFE — Polytetrafluoroethylene.

PUCK — In roller hockey, a weighted disc or ball that players try to drive into their opponents' goal.

QUAD SKATE — Refers to the original four-wheeled, rockering skate developed by James Plimpton. (See also CONVENTIONAL SKATE.)

RAMP — A wooden or metal structure used to get air. Usually two to four feet high. One variation is a spine ramp, which is two higher ramps, about four to five feet high, placed back to back.

RASPBERRY — Also known as a strawberry or a road burn, this is a skin scrape resulting from a fall.

REBOUND — The action of springing back. Rebound is the amount of energy put into the wheels and then returned, not absorbed, by the energy source.

RIPPING — In-line slang for great footwork.

ROCKERING — Lowering the middle wheel(s) to create a curved wheel line, enabling a skater to make quicker turns.

ROLLER HOCKEY — Originally played on traditional roller skates, roller hockey on in-line skates has reached widespread popularity, thanks to the Rollerblade®. Further, it offers an alternative, which is skating on a team with all the dynamics that team sports entail.

ROLLER SKATES — Originally derived from the word "skate," which means "shoot ahead or slide." A shoe with two pairs of small wheels, one attached to the heel and one to the toe.

ROLLERBLADE® — The trademarked name of the in-line skate manufacturer Rollerblade®, Inc., of Minneapolis, Minnesota. The company name, Rollerblade®, is frequently misused as both a noun and a verb to refer to the in-line skate and in-line skating, respectively. This practice is trademark infringement and its continued misuse is strongly discouraged.

ROLLERBLADING — A misnomer used to describe the in-line skating activity. Rollerblade® is a trademark.

ROTATION — The process of alternating use in a series. As with car tires, in-line wheels should be rotated to enhance their longevity and handling, especially when performing wheel-grinding stopping techniques such as the power slide.

SCALING — Peeling of the road surface.

SCULLING — A technique of skating in which skates are moved in and out, creating a continuous "S"-like movement while never leaving the ground.

SIZE — Physical magnitude. Wheel sizes range from about 67mm for some children sizes to 80mm for racing. The size represents the outside diameter, or "od" of a wheel, in millimeters.

SKATESMART — Slogan of an in-line skating safety awareness program, launched by Rollerblade®, Inc.

SKITCHING — A lazy technique inherited from skateboarders of grabbing onto the rear of a moving vehicle to receive an effortless tow. This is a dangerous practice.

SLALOM — A zigzag course created by setting up a line of cones and weaving between them.

SLIDING BOARD — An in-line training device used to work on lateral strength and to simulate side-to-side motion. May be purchased or handmade.

SNELL — Refers to the Snell Memorial Foundation, named after race car driver Pete Snell, who was killed in a car crash in the 1950s while wearing a helmet that was more decorative than functional. The foundation has its headquarters in St. James, New York. The foundation's standards for helmets made for race car drivers, motorcyclists, and bicyclists are high. Snell stickers are green or blue and have a serial number.

SPACER — A plastic or metal device in the center of the wheel to prevent the bearings from making contact with each other.

STAIR RIDING — Skating down a stairway. An advanced in-line skating technique that requires balance and stamina.

STALL — A skating technique, originally created by skateboarders, in which one reaches the upper edge of a ramp, round basin, or swimming pool and momentarily stops on the edge before initiating the descent.

STROLLER SKATING — Pushing a baby stroller while in-line skating. All-terrain strollers are recommended, as they are more stable than traditional strollers.

STYLE — In in-line skating, this relates to both fashion and technique. To be "stylin'" is to skate with exceptional technique.

SURFING — Refers to the in-line squat position with the lead leg extended. Usually used while going through a slalom.

T-STOP — A braking technique in which the non-leading leg is placed perpendicular to the leading leg, applying friction between the inner edge of the wheels and the ground. The configuration creates something similar to the letter "T".

THRASHING — Controlled skating that appears completely out of control. You will know it when you see it.

TWEAKING — Jumping and kicking your legs out to either side. Also refers to hurting the knee or back or twisting a body part.

UPHEAVAL — Localized swelling of the pavement.

USAC/RS — United States Amateur Confederation of Roller Skating.

WICKING — To remove or "wick" away moisture. Wicking socks help prevent moisture build-up on the feet.

WRIST GUARDS — Protective handwear that minimizes injury to the wrists and palms, usually the first extremities to make contact with the ground in a fall. Made of nylon, leather, neoprene, etc. Molded plastic splint guards can be built in.

Appendix
In-Line Skating Resource Guide

●●

PERIODICALS

InLine: The Skater's Magazine
2025 Pearl Street
Boulder, CO 80302
(303) 440-5111
Fax: (303) 440-3313
Founded: August 1991
Editor: Jon Lowden

InLine (controlled circulation of 40,000 copies) is published six times annually for $17.97 by InLine, Inc.

InLine is dedicated to all skaters and all segments of the sport of in-line skating, including freestyle/vert/street skating, racing and speedskating, fitness and recreational skating, roller hockey, and cross-training for other sports. In every issue, *InLine* features profiles of top skating personalities, looks at relevant safety and legal issues, and discusses training tips, skating techniques, and the latest developments in in-line technologies and ancillary products. *InLine* also lists upcoming skate races and related events whenever possible.

If you have started a new club, have an upcoming in-line competitive event, have information on roller hockey leagues, or know of a new product you would like reviewed, *InLine* would love to hear from you.

InLine, Inc. is also the publisher of *InLine Retailer and Industry News*, a publication devoted to helping the industry's dealers and manufacturers serve skaters better by reporting on the financial health of the industry, discussing and reviewing new products and product innovations, and forecasting and reporting on industry trends. *InLine Retailer* is not available by subscription, but is available free of charge to retailers and other industry notables. *InLine Retailer* is published six times a year.

Speedskating Times
2910 Northeast 11th Avenue
Pompano Beach, FL 33064
(305) 782-5928
Fax: (305) 781-4992
Founded: 1989
President and Publisher/Editor: Lauri Muir Starcevich

Speedskating Times is published eight times a year by J.L.H. Publications. Annual subscription: $25.

In 1989, Jeff Dowling (now V.P. of Marketing) and two other friends, all with ice skating backgrounds, began an ice skating club in Florida. However, the rink needed refurbishing, and they realized that they would have to raise some money.

They approached some corporations, but to no avail. They decided to try to raise the money on their own, so they launched a publication covering ice skating, the sport they had grown to love.

Says Dowling, "And here we are three years later." Ironically, they have never organized a single ice event, but have arranged dozens of in-line events. "We have definitely grown with the times." Indeed they have. In 1991, for a period of five months straight, they covered in-line skating exclusively.

Still, Jeff notes that ice and in-line skating are the only two sports he knows of that are so closely related you can play them year-round. This being the case, they hope to see their circulation climb from its steady 20,000. Although Dowling sees a big future in in-line skating, he believes that ice skating *and* in-line skating can coexist and complement each other. He tries to inform people that ice skating is a good way to work on technique, attempting to coax in-line skaters to try ice skating, just as conventional skaters eventually tried out in-line skates.

As for the future? "My goal is to make in-line skating what cycling is today — an elite competitive sport with broad appeal; to increase the prize money; and to create more exposure for both sports simultaneously." And if Jeff Dowling has anything to say about it, all of that will happen.

If you have started a new club, or have an upcoming in-line competitive event, information on roller hockey leagues, or a new product you would like reviewed, *Speedskating Times* would love to hear from you.

California Wheeling
City Sports Magazine
Northern California Office
2201 3rd Street
San Francisco, CA 94107
(415) 626-1600
Fax: (415) 621-2323
Southern California Office:
80 South Lake Avenue
Suite 500
Pasadena, CA 91101
(818) 584-9703
Fax: (818) 584-9719
Founded: 1974
Editor-in-Chief: Christopher Newbound

California Wheeling, a supplement in the back of *City Sports Magazine*, reports on bicycling and in-line skating. In addition to one or two feature articles on in-line skating, you will also find a respectable events calendar, as well as results from recent competitions.

Although $1.95 at newsstands, *City Sports* can be picked up at hundreds of sporting and lifestyle stores throughout California for free! (For home delivery, the annual subscription rate is $17.95.) Expect this supplement to grow in the future, perhaps blossoming into a full-fledged magazine.

Street Hockey Magazine
P.O. Box 55624
Sherman Oaks, CA 91413-5624
(818) 783-0979
Founded: September 1992
Editor: Kurt Helin

Street Hockey Magazine is published six times a year. Annual subscription: $18. Canadian and European subscriptions add $10.

Street Hockey Magazine is the first nationally distributed magazine devoted entirely to street hockey. Street hockey, including roller hockey, dekhockey, and floor hockey, is well situated and growing rapidly in the wake of in-line skate sales.

National newsstand distribution launched in April 1993.

The Racing Blade Magazine
Contact: Shirley Yates
1033 Shady Lane
Glen Ellyn, IL 60137
(708) 790-3230
Fax: (708) 790-3235
Founded: 1970
Editor: Robert R. Vehe

The Racing Blade is published by the Amateur Speedskating Union of the United States five times per year. Subscriptions are free to all registered members. For non-members, subscription price is $15 per year in the U.S. Subscription to Canada, South America, and Central America is $20 per year; $25 per year to Europe, Asia, and Australia.

COMPUTER RESOURCES

Once you get yourself on a pair of in-line skates, connect yourself to the nation and get on-line. Yes, it's true, there is a wealth of information to be gathered, questions to be answered, and, not least of all, enthusiasm to be shared though your personal computer.

In just five minutes on the interactive in-line/roller skating forum, topics are discussed; advice is shared; "rockering," "ABEC," and like terminology are defined; but most of all, the diverse and gregarious community of in-line skaters is brought closer together.

Although the computer often invades our privacy, it also makes the astronomical numbers and distances of the world seem less daunting, bringing us closer together. A double-edged sword? Maybe, but who cares? How else could you talk with twenty people at once, thousands of miles apart, about the finer points of wheel rotation? Think of it as a "live" national newsletter. Do whatever suits you. But stop thinking, and GET IN-LINE! by getting on-line.

INTERNET Computer Service

INTERNET is a huge global information network with sites in more than thirty countries. It is funded by various governments and organizations throughout the world that maintain INTERNET sites. What do you want to know? Computers, religion, academic subjects, hobbies, philosophy, fan clubs, music, science, sex, and yes, in-line skating — it's all here. If you are into home brewing your own beer, enjoy listening to Barry Manilow, are of Albanian descent, there is a group for one and all.

As with many things of enormous size, INTERNET is run by everyone and no one. It is virtually unmanageable. There are no committees, no politics, no organizing body, nothing signed in triplicate. It is vast — three million users. It is social — 1,800 forum news groups. There are over 900 publicly accessible sites (like telephone switching banks). INTERNET stores in excess of a million files, containing 1,000 gigabytes of information. This means that it would require two million books the size of this one to equal the amount of information available on INTERNET!

INTERNET has never been so accessible to non- university/governmental users. There are several possibilities to gain access to INTERNET. The first route is to see if your local university sells outside accounts. In essence, you use an account in the university's system that is owned by someone not directly affiliated with that university.

The second option is to access the network through a commercial bulletin board (BBS) that provides INTERNET access. The larger cities tend to have these BBS's.

Probably the cheapest avenue is to use a public access network. These are frequently referred to as Pubnets ("public network"). Pubnets are non-commercial BBS's that specialize in providing INTERNET access "to the rest of us." Charges are nominal, sometimes free.

For those who are connected with INTERNET, or have immediate access, the notation RN REC.SKATE. will give you access to the program. To receive an access list and specific connecting instructions, call the National Science Foundation Network Service Center at (617) 873-3400.

Compuserve
5000 Arlington Center Blvd.
P.O. Box 20212
Columbus, OH 43220
Customer Support: (800) 848-8990
(614) 457-8650

The Compuserve network community of over one million subscribers enjoys a vast array of features. Unlike most on-line data bases, Compuserve is affordable — starting at $8.95 per month. Arguably the most informative aspect of Compuserve is its hundreds of forums. These are special interest groups that "meet" on-line to discuss and learn about topics ranging from genealogy to software development and, yes, in-line skating.

To discover the in-line skating conference, which is held on Thursday nights at 6 p.m. Eastern Standard Time, access the Health and Fitness Forum and enter conference room #1. (Subject to change.)

ANNUAL EVENT

Athens-to-Atlanta Roller Skating Marathon
1077 Vistavia Circle
Decatur, GA 30033
(800) FOR-IISA
(404) 294-6351

This event was founded in 1981 by G. Henry Zuver III, and is the premier roller skating ultra marathon event in the country. The course spans eighty-five miles of open road between Athens and Atlanta, Georgia. The event is held every year and consistently attracts the best athletes in the sport. The race is sanctioned by the Outdoor Marathon Roller Skating Association.

Participants may register up to the day of the event for $25, but early (by mid-September) registration is recommended to ensure receiving a T-shirt. The race is held annually in mid-October.

This is the longest continually run annual event.

MANUFACTURERS

Bauer®
Canstar Sports USA, Inc.
P.O. Box 716
50 Jonergin Drive
Swanton, VT 05488
(800) 362-3146
Fax: (802) 868-4713

A manufacturer of ice skates for over sixty years, the Canadian-based Canstar Sports launched its line of in-line skates in response to the growth of in-line skating in the late '80s. They carry a complete line of roller hockey equipment.

Blackhole
P.O. Box 20
Mercer Island, WA 98404
(800) 327-9393

Manufactures bearings.

Bladetech® Corporation
3031 Columbiana-New Castle Road
New Middletown, OH 44442
(800) 238-2858

Currently offers the Bladetrainer™ in-line skate speedometer, a compact device with two buttons and a large LCD display. Its seven functions include current, average, and maximum speeds; odometer and tripmeter; stopwatch; clock; auto start-stop; and mph/kph setting. Cost is about $70.

BNQ Accessories
Contact: Steve Nash
1541 Ocean Avenue, #200
Santa Monica, CA 90401
(818) 344-2137

Offers Skate Hollerz, a completely adjustable carrying strap for in-line, roller, and ice skates. Holds two skates comfortably over a shoulder, freeing arms for better use. The Skate Hollerz is made of Velcro® and can be worn around the waist when not used for toting skates. With a choice of seven brilliant colors and cost of about $10, this is a bargain!

Bones Bearings
Powell Corp.
30 South La Patera
Santa Barbara, CA 93117
(805) 683-9091
(805) 964-0511

Manufactures bearings for skates.

Built for Speed
316 E. Seneca
Syracuse, NY 13205
(315) 492-6620

Manufactures Darkstar racing frames for Bont boots in four- and five-wheeled versions.

California Pro USA Corp.
8810 Tehco Road
San Diego, CA 92121
(619) 597-0690
(800) 932-5777
Fax: (619) 597-0776

Offers a complete line of in-line skates, protective gear, apparel, and accessories. Major innovations in in-line skate design include a "Monoshell," a one-piece boot design that eliminates the hinged upper cuff, thus providing a better fit with improved lateral control and turning power. Also invented the "Compressive Flex Air Flow System." During a stroke, the boot flexes, allowing air to pass through the liner, keeping the foot dry and comfortable.

CCM Sports Maska, Inc.
6375 Picard Street
Hyacinthe, PQ J2S 1H3
Canada
(800) 661-8225
(514) 773-5041
Fax: (514) 773-3335

CCM Sports has a joint development in an in-line skate system with Reebok®. The Reebok® Pump™ inside boot shell features custom fit and adjustable support with three buckles for multi-adjustability. Some of their features are a patented NTR® Quick Release wheels system and high rebound 77mm wheels with a 78A durometer and an aerodynamic core for a fast and smooth roll. They also manufacture the StreetSharx line of street hockey gear.

CDS Detroit
1167 Lake Point
Grosse Point Park, MI 48230
(313) 331-7371

Manufactures skid plates by retro fitting knee pads.

CYKO, L.C.
316 East 7th Street North
P.O. Box 926
Newton, IA 50208
(515) 791-2956
(800) GET-CYKO

Produces the HurricanZ in-line skate wheel.

DJ Sports
Excaliber
1201 Stonehaven Avenue
Brookfield, CO 80020
(303) 469-3699

Double Lay-R® Sock Company
62 West State Street
Doylestown, PA 18901
(800) 392-8500
(215) 340-9180
Fax: (215) 340-9183

Manufacturer of the Skate Liner (CD810) in-line skate sock, which is made of Coolmax (which holds a Dupont Certification Mark for fabrics), a channel core fiber that wicks moisture away from the foot; combats bacteria, odor and mildew; and is guaranteed to be blister-free.

Easy Street Hockey Company
3357 East Miraloma Avenue
Anaheim, CA 92806
(714) 572-0322

Offers a line of street hockey equipment.

Enrge Sports
9 Terhune Drive
Westport, CT 06880
(800) 245-9099

Enrge Sports manufactures the Enrge Backrider, which looks like a backpack but is a garment bag. It is designed to carry a complete set of business attire, including shoes and toiletries, without a wrinkle. The Backrider folds into thirds, features a padded back and shoulder straps, and comes with a pop-up leather handle so that it may be toted as a briefcase.

Two models are available: the C-420 for one ensemble or the T-1100, which holds up to five days of clothing. Prices are from $149 to $199.

Etto®
Etto AB
Riddargaten 12, Box 5310
S-102 46
Stockholm, Sweden
46 (0) 8 662 99 66
Fax: 46 (0) 8 611 57 73

This Swedish company has been developing bicycle helmets, which can also be used for in-line skating, for ten years. They offer models for every age and style. The unique patented shell features the ability to adjust for exact sizing. The helmets are imported and available throughout the U.S. Prices begin at $79.

Excelsior Inline Frames
607 Atlantic Avenue
Fort Pierce, FL 34950
(800) 942-6805
(407) 465-1162

Excelsior In-line Frames is the only manufacturer of a one-piece axle system that eliminates the need to line up washers and spaces. Made so that both the left and right frame axles face toward the inside, thus allowing fast and easy wheel changes. The signature five-wheel frame weighs 7.5 ounces.

Falcon Sports
817 Cedar Falls Road
Menomonie, WI 54751
(715) 235-8830
Fax: (715) 235-8875

Falcon Sports offers various hockey and street sticks.

Fitmax
150 Mitchell Blvd.
San Raphael, CA 94903
(800) 756-7779
(415) 499-0841
Fax: (415) 472-5540

Fitmax has a complete line of protective gear. They also carry the Ultra-Wheel brand in-line skates and accessories, as well as street hockey accessories. Mail order is available.

Franklin Sports Industries Inc.
17 Campanelli Parkway
P.O. Box 508
Stoughton, MA 02072
(617) 344-1111

Franklin Sports offers a complete line of street/roller hockey equipment.

Goal-Eez Sports Nets Corp.
2586 Dunwin Drive, Unit 1
Mississauga, Ontario
Canada L5L 1J5
(416) 820-2499
(416) 820-5142

This company offers premium quality goal nets, which are made of high-strength plastic that withstands extreme temperatures and can be used with any type of puck. They currently offer four different models.

Grip® Inline Speed Control™
825 Pearl Street, Suite C
Boulder, CO 80302
(303) 444-4999
(303) 444-2220

Manufactures a hand-held braking system.

Interapps
Kazaz Inc.
447 Grand Avenue, Suite 1
St. Paul, MN 55102
(612) 224-5700
(800) 257-3550

Manufactures Rapps racing skates.

Hyper Inline
15241 Transistor Lane
Huntington Beach, CA 92649
(714) 373-3300
Fax: (714) 373-2525

Hyper Inline currently offers a full line of in-line wheels — recreation, hockey, performance, and both indoor and outdoor racing wheels. Height — 64mm to 82mm; Durometer — 75A to 93A.

Karhu USA Inc.
P.O. Box 4249
South Burlington, VT 05406
(802) 864-4519

Manufactures the Koho Street Revolution line of street hockey gear.

Kinetic
6507 Cecilia Drive
Minneapolis, MN 55433
(612) 941-1916
(612) 941-8944 Fax

Manufactures an interchangeable ice and in-line frame. Rotating the wheels only requires switching the frames.

Kneedspeed®
2200-4 NW Birdsdale
Gresham, OR 97030
(800) 523-7674
(503) 666-9275 (in Oregon)
Fax: (503) 661-4298

Manufacturer of a slide board designed to improve cardiovascular strength. It improves lateral speed and agility by strengthening the pelvic girdle and lower extremities. Kneedspeed® offers two portable configurations (Model M60 at 6 feet and Model M80 at 8 feet), as well as a professional model, the M100 at 8 feet.

Maska U.S.
P.O. Box 381
Pierson Industrial Park
Bradford, VT 05033
(800) 451-4600

This is the U.S. subsidiary of CCM Sport Maska, Inc.

Mylec Inc.
Mill Circle Road
Winchendon Springs, MA 01447
(508) 297-0089

Offers a full range of street/roller hockey equipment. A brochure is available upon request for $3.

NordicTrack
141 Jonathon Blvd. North
Chaska, MN 55318
(800) 336-5357
(612) 448-6120

NordicTrack distributes the Kneespeed® slide board, which is designed to improve cardiovascular strength as well as lateral speed and agility by strengthening the pelvic girdle and lower extremities. The portable configuration is available for $129. They also distribute the Slide Basics video by Kneespeed® (VHS, 30 minutes, $19.95).

NüSkate™ Inc.
Morgan Avenue South
Suite 3
Minneapolis, MN 55431
(800) 800-8740
Fax: (612) 881-2421

NüSkate carries a full line of in-line skates and accessories, offering the products to the consumer at a low cost on a direct mail basis. They are the developer of Flites™, a carbon fiber frame designed for high-performance skating. NüSkate will fit Bont and Zandstra boots, and will accommodate up to 80mm wheels. Cost is $129.95 per pair.

NZ Manufacturing, Inc.
6644 South 196th Place, Suite T-106
Kent, WA 98032-2124
(206) 251-1485
Fax: (206) 251-0934

This manufacturer of StretchCordz™ training equipment currently offers three products (Speed Skating Turn Cable, Modular Turn Cable, and Super Turn Cable) for speed skating cross-training. These products are designed to simulate the feeling an ice skater experiences while traveling around a turn on an ice arena.

Paragon Racing Products
690 Industrial Circle South
Shakopee, MN 55379
(612) 496-0091
Fax: (612) 496-0191

Paragon Racing Products currently offers Skatelites™ (formerly Bladelites), which are best described as headlights for your skates. Skatelites™ emit a bright, focusable light in front of the skates, improving the skater's ability to see and be seen by others. The product includes mounting hardware and two lights. Forthcoming products include training gear for the speed skater and other accessories.

Performance Inc.
(What's Up With Skates)
1 Performance Way
Box 2741
Chapel Hill, NC 27514
(919) 933-9113
(919) 942-5431 Fax

Manufactures a leather boot with one to five wheels.

Revolution Inline
15905 NE 31st Avenue
Ridgefield, WA 98642
(206) 573-2093
Contact: Bryen Hansen

Revolution Inline is a low volume manufacturer of high performance racing wheels that feature replaceable "wheels." In other words, instead of replacing the whole wheel, you replace the outer tread only.

Riedell Shoes Inc.
P.O. Box 21
122 Cannon River Avenue
Red Wing, MN 55066
(612) 388-8251
Fax: (612) 388-8616

Riedell Shoes currently offers two inline racing boot models and two recreational models. The top-of-the-line racing boot features the "Thermal Sensitive" Padding System for immediate comfort through fast break-in materials and a built-in power strap.

Recreational boots feature a computer-designed poly shell that creates an extremely strong and lightweight boot. The hockey boot also features the "Thermal Sensitive" Padding System, which reacts to body temperature for an excellent fit.

Roller Derby Skate Corporation
311 West Edwards Street
Litchfield, IL 62056
(217) 324-3961

The Roller Derby Skate Corporation was founded in 1937. They distribute Roller Derby brand in-line skates as well as ice and quad skates. These skates can be found at Sears, JCPenney, Walmart, etc.

Rollerblade®, Inc.
5101 Shady Oak Road
Minneapolis, MN 55343
(800) 232-ROLL
Fax: (612) 930-7100
(800) 68-BLADE (Event-Line)

This is the company that started the in-line explosion in 1982. Offers a full line of in-line skates, protective equipment, and accessories.

Skating categories include fitness, recreation, cross-training, and high performance (racing and competition). Rollerblade® also carries a complete line of in-line hockey equipment.

Rollerguard, Inc.
81 Major Mackenzie Drive East
Richmond Hill, Ontario L4C 1H2
Canada
(416) 508-5759
Fax: (416) 770-0360

Rollerguard manufactures a device that covers skate wheels and allows the skater to walk with the ease of shoes. When not in use, Rollerguard fastens to the back of the skate. They are ideal for rain and wet pavement, and are available in numerous sizes for under $20.

See Mee
11 Martense Court
Brooklyn, NY 11226
(718) 469-0358

See Mee manufactures a round 2.5-inch fluorescent button. It reflects strong light up to 100 feet and can be seen day and night. Available in assorted brilliant colors.

Skate Action
Skate Action Sports
P.O. Box 2676
Stamford, CT 06906
(800) 398-1911 (24 hours)

Skate Action carries an extensive line of in-line clothing — shirts, tank tops, shorts,

and caps — in an array of vibrant colors. Prices range from $10 to $20 plus shipping costs.

Stevens Creek Software
21346 Rumford Drive
Cupertino, CA 95014
(408) 725-0424

This company offers a multi-sport software package designed to record, plan, and analyze training and races. The program is Macintosh and IBM compatible, can include custom entries, and is loaded with features.

Sun Hockey, Inc.
P.O. Box 36155
Pentagon Towers
Edina, MN 55435
(800) 933-PUCK

Sun Hockey offers an innovative street and roller hockey puck, called Hot Pucks™, as well as additional hockey equipment.

Sure-Grip International
5519 Rawlings Street
Southgate, CA 90280
(310) 923-0724
(310) 923-1160 Fax

Manufactures the Airlite frame.

Thunderwear®, Inc.
Calle 1060-C Negocio
San Clemente, CA 92672
(714) 492-1141
(800) 422-6565
Fax: (714) 492-3259

Thunderwear offers a variety of skating safety wear, as well as gloves and footwear for virtually every California lifestyle activity. New Glove/Wrist Guards are made of 2mm neoprene with an Amara and super-strength Kevlar palm. Mold plastic splints guard against injury (Model T-688). Available in a solid black or black/purple combination. XS-XL.

Knee and elbow pads are made with Cordura and heavy-duty polyurethane caps held by reinforced grommets.

Twincam Bearings
Twincam Precision In-Line Components
1123 Riverside Drive
Broomsdale, MN 55337
(800) 238-9457
(612) 890-6368
Manufactures bearings.

Ultralube
Contact: Milo Smith
M & A Smith Corp.
421 North 2nd Street
Wormleysburg, PA 17043
(717) 763-9562
Fax: (717) 763-1836
This company offers Ultralube lubrication formulas for precision bearings. Also available is Ultralube for processed bearings. Additional items include bearing tubes, wheel tubes, bearing pullers, bearing presses, and hub remover cups. The lubrication formula and processed bearings were developed through extensive research and testing against virtually every other product on the market.

Ultra-Wheels®
First Team Sports, Inc.
2274 Woodale Drive
Mounds View, MN 55112-4900
(800) 458-2250
(612) 780-4454
Fax: (612) 780-8908
First Team Sports, Inc. is currently the only publicly traded company in the in-line skating industry (NASDAQ FTSP). They manufacture a complete line of Ultra-Wheel® in-line skates (thirteen models at press time), street hockey equipment, protective wear, and in-line skating accessories.
The Gretzky Wings Air Comprex (Wayne Gretzky signature model) features a patented

air replacement system, an adjustable rocker, and a reinforced Vandar frame.

WindSkate®, Inc.
P.O. Box 3081
Santa Monica, CA 90403
(310) 453-4808
Fax: (310) 829-9511
WindSkate® is the designer of skate sail devices. They manufacture and sell a range of windskating devices for in-line skates, roller skates, and skateboards. Modifications in sail and skate equipment permit virtually all-terrain WindSkate® activity—pavement, desert, beach, and snow.
Hand-held in-line and roller skate sails include Bladesail, a high-performance Roller WindSkate® Dacron® sail, with aluminum rigging and a padded apex for knees. For novices and pros in light to moderate winds.

Yak Research
850 West McArthur
Oakland, CA 94608
(800) 488-YAKS
(510) 652-0893
Yak Research offers a skating slideboard, which helps to build speed and endurance. Two sizes are offered: 2' x 8' and 2' x 10'. A training video is also available. This mail order company is open twenty-four hours a day.

Zandstra Sports
Postbus 150
AC Joure
Holland
031-5138-15858
Fax: 031-5138-16415
A long-time manufacturer of the ice speed skate, Zandstra introduced the Zandstra Skeeler primarily as a dry-land cross-trainer for ice speed skating, hockey, and skiing. Several models are offered. They are geared toward the in-line speed skating, recreational

and novice categories. The Zandstra Skeeler features a lightweight aluminum frame, 80mm wheels, and a superior design. Molded or leather boots are available. All accessories, including safety equipment, are offered in the current product line. Prices begin in the high $200 range.

RETAILERS

Note: In the following section, the ✪ symbol indicates Certified IISA Instructor.

Arizona

Hockey Hut
55 East Broadway
Tempe, AZ 85282
(602) 967-5219

California

Action Sports
8200 Stockdale Hwy., #B3
Bakersfield, CA 93311
(805) 833-4000

Amcan Sports
4545 Sepulveda Blvd.
Culver City, CA 90230
(310) 391-0539

Other location:
6023 ³/₄ Reseda Blvd.
Tarzana, CA 91356
(818) 345-6156

Any Mountain Skates ✪
71 Tamal Vista
Corte Madera, CA 94925
(415) 927-0170

Carries in-line skates and accessories and offers skate rentals and a basic training clinic.

Other locations:
1975 Diamond Blvd.
Concord, CA 94520
(510) 674-0174

490 Marketplace
San Ramon, CA 94583
(510) 275-1010
10495 North De Anza Blvd.
Cupertino, CA 95014
(408) 255-6162

Bud's Pro Skate
16942 Beach Blvd.
Huntington Beach, CA 91760
(714) 843-6922

C.A.E. Sporting Goods
148 South Glendora Avenue
West Covina, CA 91790
(818) 919-1933

Courtesy Sports ✪
4856 El Camino Real
Los Altos, CA 94022
(800) 729-1771 (Orders)
(415) 968-7970 (Information)
Fax: (415) 968-4609

Carries a complete line of in-line skates and accessories from all major manufacturers. Call for a store catalog.

D & D Sporting Goods
4245 ¹/₂ Woodruff Avenue
Lakewood, CA 90713
(310) 429-9633

Dales Scoreboard Sports
969 West Foothill Blvd.
Claremont, CA 91711
(714) 621-9493

Demo-Ski
509-B Francisco Blvd.
San Raphael, CA 94901
(415) 454-3500

Features rentals and sales of top-of-the-line in-line skates, snow skis, snowboards, and waterskiing equipment. Displays a wide variety of men's, women's, and children's in-line skates, racing accessories, roller hockey equipment, and protective gear. Special orders are accepted for specialty racing skates and other in-line skates that are uncommon to stock.

Encore Sports
1789 Thousand Oaks Blvd.
Thousands Oaks, CA 91362
(805) 379-0020
Other location:
22715 Ventura Blvd.
Woodland Hills, CA 91362
(818) 348-8813

FTC Sports
1586 Bush Street
San Francisco, CA 94109
(415) 673-8663

Go Skate
2306 L Almaden Road
San Jose, CA 95125
(408) 978-6487
Other locations:
601 Beach Street
Santa Cruz, CA 95060
(408) 425-1958
1554 Saratoga Avenue
P-405
San Jose, CA 95129
(408) 378-1958
7630 Fairoaks Blvd., #D
Carmichael, CA 95608
(916) 944-2753

Gold Coast Skate and Surf
7036 Greenleaf Avenue
Whittier, CA 90601
(310) 698-5154

Golden Bear Skate Shop
2383 West Lomita Blvd.
Lomita, CA 90717
(310) 534-3100
Other location:
10712 Washington Blvd.
Los Angeles, CA 90232
(310) 838-6611

Gremic's SK8's
15349 Los Gatos Blvd.
Los Gatos, CA 95032
(408) 358-1169

Herb Bauer Sporting Goods
6264 North Blackstone Avenue
Fresno, CA 93710
(209) 323-6762

Hudson Bay Inline
5405 College Avenue
Oakland, CA 94618
(800) 447-0400
(510) 658-9622

Specializes in wheels, bearings, and axle systems only. Store open seven days a week; mail order available twenty-four hours a day.

Lombardi Sports
152 Clement Street
San Francisco, CA 94118
(415) 387-0600

M Sports
80 Hegenberger Loop
Oakland, CA 64621
(510) 339-9313

Montclair Sports
1970 Mountain Blvd.
Oakland, CA 94611
(510) 339-9313

Morningstar Surf and Sport
195 South Turnpike Road
Santa Barbara, CA 93111
(805) 967-8288

Neilands Hockey Experts
185 South Euclid, #20
Pasadena, CA 91106
(818) 577-2332

Nuvo Colours
1600 South El Camino Real
San Mateo, CA 94403
(415) 571-1537

A California Lifestyle Store. Offers rentals, sales, training, and full service. An exclusive retailer of Rollerblade® in-line skates, but also carries various lines of skating apparel. Hours: Monday to Friday — 10 a.m. to 7 p.m.; Saturday — 9 a.m. to 7 p.m.; Sunday — 9 a.m. to 6 p.m.

Other locations:

3108 Fillmore Street
San Francisco, CA 94123
(415) 771-NUVO

45 East Main Street
Los Gatos, CA 95032
(408) 395-6006

Precision Sports
10611 Acacia Avenue
Garden Grove, CA 92640
(714) 539-9901

Exclusive retailer of La Beda in-line wheels.

Roll With It
920 Manhattan Avenue
Manhattan Beach, CA 90266
(310) 379-9071

Carries Rollerblade®, Bauer®, and Switch It® brand in-line skates. Offers sales, service, repairs, rentals, demonstrations; call for information. Special group and weekly rental rates. Hockey equipment, videos, and books are also available. Free catalog.

Shore Sport Inc.
550 Deep Valley Drive
Rolling Hills, CA 90274
(310) 439-7250

Other location:
5209 East 2nd Street
Long Beach, CA 90803
(310) 439-7250

Skate Pro Sports
2555 Irving Street
San Francisco, CA 94122
(415) 752-8776
Fax: (415) 752-8781

A full service, exclusive retailer of in-line skate products. Carries ice skating, speed skating, in-line skating, and roller hockey equipment. Gives a free two-hour group lesson with the purchase of skates. In-line rentals are available at $5 an hour or $20 a day (includes protective gear). Group and private lessons are also available, as well as custom design and repairs.

Skates On Haight ✪
1818 Haight Street
San Francisco, CA 94117
(800) 554-1235 (Orders)
(415) 224-9800 (Information)
(415) 752-8375 (In-line skates)
Fax: (415) 873-0200

Nationwide mail order is available. Call for a free catalog. Carries all major brands of in-line skates, as well as hockey equipment, apparel, and accessories.

Other location:
384 Oyster Point Blvd., #5
San Francisco, CA 94080

Spectrum Sports
15504 La Mirada Blvd.
La Mirada, CA 90638
(714) 523-7100

Sporting Ideas
1531 West Redondo Beach Blvd.
Gardena, CA 90247
(310) 516-7873

Sportlife
514 3rd Street
Davis, CA 95616
(916) 758-6000

Sports Fever ☻
73360 Hwy. 111, #4
Palm Desert, CA 92260
(619) 340-0252

Tameku Sports
30520 Rancho California Drive, #108
Temecula, CA 92591
(714) 695-4422

Team Karim
2801 Telegraph Avenue
Berkeley, CA 94705
(415) 841-2181

Send $3 for catalogs and decals. A distributor for Poolsport/Eddy Matzger Special and Force Series: Brute Force and Peloton Force. Open six days a week. Call first for Sunday hours of operation.

Val Surf and Sport
4810 Whitsett Avenue
North Hollywood, CA 91617
(818) 769-6977

Other locations:
22211 Ventura Blvd.
Woodland Hills, CA 91364
(818) 888-6488
3055 East Thousand Oaks Blvd.
Thousand Oaks, CA 91362
(808) 497-1166

Willows Skate and Surf
1431 Park Street
Alameda, CA 94501
(510) 523-5566

In-line sales, service, and rentals. Carries all major brands and protective equipment. Free lessons are available.

WindSkate®, Inc.
P.O. Box 3081
Santa Monica, CA 90403
(310) 453-4808
Fax: (310) 829-9511

The originators of skate sail devices. Manufactures and sells a range of sail skating devices for in-line skates, roller skates, and skateboards. Modifications in sail and skate equipment permit virtually all-terrain WindSkate® activity — pavement, desert, beach, snow. Hand-held in-line and roller skate sails include Bladesail, with a high performance roller Windskate® Dacron® sail, aluminum rigging, and padded apex for knees. For novices and pros in light to moderate winds.

Windsurf Bicycle Warehouse
428 South Airport Blvd.
San Francisco, CA 94118
(415) 588-1714

Carries several major brands of in-line skates and accessories.

Colorado

SportFix
Beach Street/Rocky Mountain Marine
5411 Leetsdale Drive
Denver, CO 80222
(800) 466-5463 (Mail order)
(303) 399-2824
Fax: (303) 399-2842

Carries Rollerblade®, Bauer®, Ultra-Wheels, California Pro, and Bont brand in-line skates. Rentals are available. Low price guarantee. Call for details.

Other location:
1521 Pearl Street
Boulder, CO 80302
(303) 444-2333

Sports Plus
1055 South Gaylord
Denver, CO 80209

Connecticut

High Gear Action Sports
72 Main Street
Westport, CT 06880
(203) 221-7711

Carries in-line skates and accessories.

Florida

Wide World Sporting Goods
220 South University Drive
Plantation, FL 33324
(305) 475-9800

Idaho

Action Sports of Idaho
214 South 15th Street
Boise, ID 83702
(208) 383-0073

Pro Fit Sports
750 Main Street
Boise, ID 83702
(208) 338-1222

Illinois

Rainbo Sports
5920 West Dempster
Morton Grove, IL 60053
(708) 470-0323

Carries an enormous inventory of Rollerblade® skates and accessories. Test "rolls" offered prior to purchase. Has a full service repair shop. Offers worldwide mail order service.

Other location:
4836 North Clark Street
Chicago, IL 60640
(312) 275-5500

Kansas

Adventure Sports
10922 West 24 Terrace
Shawnee, KS 66203
(913) 962-2323

Other location:
6249 East 21st Street, #100
Wichita, KS 67208
(316) 689-8051

Raleighs Bike Source
11912 West 119th Street
Overland Park, KS 66213
(913) 451-1515

RC Sports, Inc.
9910 Lakeview
Lenexa, KS 66219
(800) 752-8311

Carries every major brand and many lesser-known brands of in-line skates and accessories.

Kentucky

Pro Quality Skate
1774 Bardstown Road
Louisville, KY 40205
(502) 451-8298

Skate Station
3320 Frankfort Avenue
Louisville, KY 40206
(502) 895-4532

Massachusetts

Burt's Sports
Cranberry Plaza
East Wareham, MA 02538
(508) 295-9165

Other location:
850 Main Street
Falmouth, MA 02540
(508) 540-0644

Sigers Sports
10 Technology Drive
Hudson, MA 01749
(508) 562-4404

Sparky's Sports
300 Broadway
Methuen, MA 01844
(508) 689-9511

Michigan

Ace Hanses Hardware
In-line Skates and Accessories
22105 West Warren
Dearborn Heights, MI 48127
(313) 562-0505

  Carries in-line skates and accessories.

Harpar Sport Shop
17157 Harpar
Detroit, MI 48224
(313) 885-5390
(313) 885-4995

  Features Bauer® and Rollerblade® skates and accessories.

Minnesota

Bill St. Mans Sporting Goods
4159 28th Avenue South
Minneapolis, MN 55406
(612) 722-1447

Dave's Sporting Goods
1021 East Moore Lake Drive
Fridley, MN 55432
(612) 571-4110

Westwood Sports
9601 Garfield Avenue South
Minneapolis, MN 55420
(612) 881-2222

Missouri

Hockey Loft
11608 Olive Street
Creve Coeur, MO 63141
(314) 567-3719

Nevada

Excell Skates
235 East Plum
Reno, NV 89502
(702) 322-6001

Shoreline Ski and Sports
P.O. Box 5936
Stateline, NV 89449
(702) 588-8777

New Jersey

Skate's Edge Hockey Superstores
311 White Horse Pike
Magnolia, NJ 08049
(609) 784-7555

New Mexico

Skate City Supply
P.O. Box 379
Cedar Crest, NM 87008
(505) 281-5513
(505) 294-6699

  Only professional skate shop with a full line of in-line skates in New Mexico. Sells and rents in-line skates, roller skates, skateboards, snowboards, and Nordic skis. Also sells ratchet buckles to improve the fit of in-line boots.

New York

County Sports
2993 Hempstead Turnpike
Levittown, NY 11756
(516) 731-7970

Dante Cossi Sports
2600 Newbridge Road
Bellmore, NY 11710
(516) 783-0215

High Gear Action Sports
59 Purchase Street
Rye, NY 10580
(914) 967-0252

    Carries in-line skates and accessories.

Paragon Sports
867 Broadway
New York, NY 10003
(212) 255-8036

Peck and Goodie Skates
917 8th Avenue
New York, NY 10019
(212) 246-6123

Sneaks and Sports
3904 Richmond Avenue
Staten Island, NY 10312
(718) 845-1800

Sport Depot
156-40C Crossbay Blvd.
Howard Beach, NY 11414
(718) 845-1800

Sport Scene
2776 Sunrise Hwy.
Bellmore, NY 11710
(516) 826-6300

Wolf's Sporting Goods
221 Sunrise Hwy.
Rockville Center, NY 11570
(516) 766-5328

North Carolina

Morgan's Cycle and Fitness
2513 Sunset Avenue
Rocky Mount, NC 27804
(919) 443-4480

Ohio

Bladz
4378 Mayfield Road
South Euclid, OH 44121
(216) 382-7587

Cleveland Sport
4983 Ridgeberry Blvd.
Lynnhearst, OH 44124
(216) 382-8980

Cleveland Sporting Goods
4452 Mayfield Road
South Euclid, OH 44121
(216) 842-5241

Frische Jim Sports
5842 Ridge Road
Parma, OH 44129
(216) 842-5241

Oregon

Coyards Sport and Hockey
8835 SW Canyon Lane, #135N
Portland, OR 97225
(503) 297-5449

ICU Skate Co.
79 SW First Street
Portland, OR 97209
(800) 796-2336
(503) 497-9083
Fax: (503) 497-1009

    Importer of Raps and Mogema frames.
Mail order is available.

Pennsylvania

Shady Skates
7501 Penn Avenue, Point Breeze
Pittsburgh, PA 15208
(412) 731-5400

South Carolina

Vans and Stuff Skate Shop ✪
946 Orlean Road
Charleston, SC 29407
(803) 571-3244

Other location:
320 West Coleman
Mt. Pleasant, SC 29464
(803) 884-1312

Texas

Armadillo Sports ✪
1800 Barton Springs Road
Austin, TX 78704
(512) 478-4128

Carey's Sporting Goods
5800 L Camp Bowie Blvd.
Fort Worth, TX 76107
(817) 735-4794

Flatlander Ski and Sport
1750 Alma Road, #122
Richardson, TX 75081
(214) 690-4579

Skate-Tex Inc.
310 S.E. 4th Street
Grand Prairie, TX 75051
(214) 262-8349

Utah

Bike, Board, and Blade
8801 South 700 East
Sandy, UT 84070
(801) 561-2626

Washington

Angle Lake Cyclery & Fitness
31821 Gateway Blvd. South
Gateway Center
Federal Way, WA 98003
(206) 839-4632

Carries a complete line of in-line skates and accessories. Also offers full service repairs and skating rentals. Publishes *Inline Info* newsletter.

Bridgeport Cyclery and Fitness
8819 Bridgeport Way
Tacoma, WA 98499
(206) 588-2245

CLUBS

Note: In the following section, the ✪ symbol indicates Certified IISA Instructor.

Alabama

Competition Skates
Contact: John Skelton
501 Springville
Birmingham, AL 35215
(205) 854-9617

Arizona

University of Arizona Skaters Club
Contact: Lisa Toole
Tucson, AZ
(602) 623-2632

California

Chico Skate Club
Contact: Danny McGee
726 West 2nd Avenue, #E
Chico, CA 95826
(916) 342-2223

Golden Gate Park Skaters
Contact: David Miles
1855 Oak Street
San Francisco, CA 94117
(415) 681-7948

Nor-Cal Skeelers
Contact: Rick Babington
2200 Coffee Road, #89
Modesto, CA 95355
(209) 524-7928

Florida

Central Florida Lightning
Contact: John C. Morrisey
222 Tallgate Trail
Orlando, FL 32750
(407) 767-5641

Tampa Bay Road Rollers
Contact: Bill Fussel
P.O. Box 0682
Ozona, FL 33601
(813) 786-5138

Georgia

Atlanta Peachtree Road Warriors ☉
Contact: G. Henry Zuver III
1094 Piedmont Avenue N.E.
Atlanta, GA 30309
(404) 525-8609

Hawaii

Oahu Inline Skate Team ☉
Contact: Dan Seiden
909 Coolidge Street, #203
Honolulu, HI 96826
(808) 944-8970

Idaho

Boise In-Line Skaters Club
Contact: Beau Parent and Kurt Snieder
P.O. Box 774
Boise, ID 83701-0074
(208) 338-1222

Illinois

Windy City Road Rollers
Contact: Milan Mitrovic
P.O. Box 46492
Chicago, IL 60646
(312) 775-4681

Indiana

Indy In-Line Skate Club
Contact: Brad Hughey
355 Winding Way
Carmel, IN 46032
(317) 848-9410

Maryland

Baltimore Street Skaters
Contact: Hal Ashman
2418 York Road
Baltimore, MD 21093
(410) 666-9463

Massachusetts

Boston Blades
Box 63
Prudential Center
Boston, MA 02199
(617) 267-6639

Michigan

City Rollers ☉
15820 Windmill Point Drive
Grosse Point Park, MI 48230
(313) 824-0011

Currently the largest in-line skating club in the country, boasting 1200 members and averaging fifty new members per month. Co-founded in July 1991 by Mark Farnen and Mary Pittman. Monthly newsletter covers in-line skating news, profiles, member-only equipment "bargains," and a calendar of events. Cites reason for huge appeal as the huge variety of activities and membership benefits.

Missouri

St. Louis In-Line Skating Association
Contact: Gregory Issiff
St. Louis, MO
(314) 427-5963

New York

New York Road Skaters Association
Contact: Steve Novak
328 East 94th Street
New York, NY 10128
(212) 534-7790

Roller Derby Training Center
Contact: Dianne Goldberg
230 West 79th Street, Apt. 52
New York, NY 10024

North Carolina

Charlotte Blade Rollerz ✪
Contact: Jack Wilson
505 3-B North Graham
Charlotte, NC 28202
(704) 344-1555

Oklahoma

Tulsa Inline Animals
Contact: Brian Richardson
4321 S. Birmingham Drive
Tulsa, OK 74105
(918) 744-7175

Pennsylvania

Bladin' Action ✪
Contact: Jennifer Goldstein
224 S. Broad Street
Philadelphia, PA 19102
(215) 731-0977

Texas

Houston Skate This! Club
Contact: Dan Mattutat
Houston, TX
(713) 528-6102

Houston Urban Animals
Contact: John McKay
Houston, TX
(713) 528-6102

Interplanetary Inline Skate Coalition
Contact: David Tyler and Darren Jenks
P.O. Box 5003
Amarillo, TX 79159
(806) 371-3020

Washington

Angle Lake Speed Team
Contact: Jerry Suhrstedt
31821 Gateway Blvd., South
Federal Way, WA 98003
(206) 839-4632

IISA-CERTIFIED INSTRUCTORS

Alberta, Canada

Edmonton
Kelly Brooks
(403) 432-0309

Arizona

Phoenix
Kevin Chadwick,
Tammy Johnson
(602) 493-0999

Scottsdale
Steve Clauter
(602) 280-6985
Steve Jelacic III
(602) 860-8421
Steve Jelacic IV
(602) 391-1139
Bob Labine
(602) 266-6233

Tempe
Ray Pisar, Diana Toone
(602) 831-2166

British Columbia, Canada

Vancouver
RollerDave Dickey
(604) 689-8987
Ken Lee
(604) 874-9801

California

Agoura
Tom Williams
(805) 372-5138

Alameda
Kevin C. Farrell
(510) 652-7827

Concord
Chris Pilgram
(510) 674-0714

Costa Mesa
Konstantin Ammossow
(714) 645-7655
Jeff Jochum
(714) 642-4688

Cupertino
Todd Neilson
(408) 255-6162

Dixon
Jeff Carlisle
(206) 678-1104

Encinitas
Mike Cornell
(619) 634-0372
David Grimsrud
(619) 755-6299

Larkspur
Serge Rigo
(415) 927-7049

Laguna Beach
Chris Parnell
(714) 497-4962

Monterey
Steve Dodge
(408) 372-1807

Moorpark
Walt Collins
(805) 529-9883

Newport Beach
Rene Bruce
(714) 650-8885

Oakland
Jim Essick
(510) 273-9422

Palm Desert
Rick Vincent
(619) 340-0252

Palo Alto
Ben Bakst
(415) 323-9115
Leila Haletky
(415) 325-0814

San Francisco
Carol Sloan
(415) 244-9800

San Jose
Delion Cummings
(408) 257-5456
Geoff Nelson
(408) 255-6162

San Roman
John Walsh
(510) 275-1010

Santa Barbara
Joanne Bahura
(805) 965-6676

Santa Monica
Jill Schulz
(800) 965-6676

Santa Rosa
Linda Illsley
(707) 545-0373
David Kent
(707) 539-6263
Chartelle Tarrant
(707) 538-2823

Thousand Oaks
Jim DeMattia
(805) 497-1906

Topanga
Chris Morris
(310) 455-2523

Union City
Liz Miller
(510) 471-1953

Colorado

Boulder
Bruce Gamble
(303) 443-0715

Denver
Tim Dixon
(303) 721-9435
Mike Foster
(303) 722-3424

Englewood
Aaron Garfield
(303) 771-0089

Ft. Collins
Clint Eccher
(303) 221-1915
Andy Milewski
(303) 482-1069

Littleton
Ginger Conrad
(303) 290-6505

Silverthorne
Mary Russell
(303) 262-0736

Connecticut
New Haven
Ellen Bulger
(203) 389-4921

Delaware
Newark
Ron Amores
(302) 368-5707

District of Columbia
Jack Murphy
(703) 560-7586

Florida
Apopka
Tina Salafatinos
(407) 880-3828

Davie
Desmond Kameka
(305) 766-8806

Del Ray Beach
Tom Baker,
Arlene Malloch
(407) 495-8326

Ft. Lauderdale
George Batchelor
(305) 467-2822
Robert Lumbard
(305) 764-8800

Gainesville
Petrie
(904) 373-7873

Longwood
Ken Wagoner
(407) 332-8413

Miami
Robert Cedeno
(305) 667-8643

Miami Beach
Kalinda Aaron
(305) 933-6113

North Miami Beach
Stan Wong
(305) 944-3240

Ocala
Doug Chucian
(904) 694-7345

Sarasota
Mitzi Livingston
(813) 922-3284

West Palm Beach
Tracy Stalnaker
(407) 471-8867

Georgia
Duluth
Devon Peteet
(404) 888-3591

Roswell
Tammy Kesting
(404) 415-SKAT

Hawaii
Aiea
Mike Temple,
Tim Temple,
Daniel Dennissen Jr.
(808) 487-5283

Illinois
Evanston
Gail Shrawder
(708) 864-9306

Lake Forest
Steve Boersma
(708) 381-7559

Northbrook
Mark Pieters
(708) 272-7655

Palatine
Brooks Goldade
(708) 381-7559

Schaumburg
Justin Brooks
(708) 925-8527

Indiana
Ft. Wayne
Greg Allen
(219) 422-1316
Gregg Caley
(219) 436-7655

Kentucky
Louisville
Mike Van Hamburg
(502) 451-4395

Massachusetts
Boston
Cole
(617) 356-2510
Duane Lucia
(617) 248-3838

Braintree
Aaron Transki
(617) 356-2510

Natick
Chris Roberts
(508) 651-1163

Stoneham
George P. Canning
(617) 438-9086

Maryland

Gaithersburg
Benny Christakis
(301) 926-0730

Hunt Valley
Paul Harris
(410) 527-1972

Street
Terri Higginbothom
(410) 836-0407

Michigan

Dearborn
David R. Cooper
(313) 478-9579

Farmington Hills
John McLellan
(313) 478-9597

Highland Park
Ervin Johnson
(313) 867-3129

Royal Oak
Mark Aisuss
(313) 542-6709
Kurt Martin
(313) 258-5188

Minnesota

Afton
Jim Heldt
(612) 436-5528

Eagan
John Glynn
(612) 688-2344

Minneapolis
Laurie Hutton
(612) 623-1850
Dean Kaese
(612) 924-2348
Trevor Miyamoto
(612) 930-7000
Chris Nelms,
George Nelms
(612) 944-7181
Dave Nelson
(612) 922-1141
Tom Reinke
(612) 623-8026

North Oaks
Julie Wild
(612) 490-0326

St. Paul
Elby Cossette
(612) 930-7804

Nebraska

Ponca
Dan Martin
(402) 755-4120

New Mexico

Albuquerque
Tim Cone
(505) 268-4876

New York

Bronxville
Doug Grigg
(914) 946-0404

New York
Richard Hood
(212) 869-3050
Joel Rappelfeld
(212) 744-4444

St. Belle Harbor
Robert McHale
(718) 634-6874

Syracuse
John Roadarmel
(315) 445-1392

White Plains
Kirsten Fuerst
(914) 428-3516
Mindy Moyer
(914) 946-8504

North Carolina

Charlotte
John Severson
(704) 366-2053
Jack Wilson
(704) 344-1555

Ohio

Dublin
Pete Lipovsek
(614) 889-9437

Parma
Adrian Szendel
(216) 888-3678

Ontario, Canada

Brampton
Dan Genge
(416) 840-1944

London
Jennifer Potts
(519) 858-0718

Toronto
Nancy Jakemouska
(613) 567-2368

Oregon
Bend
Jack Hart
(503) 382-1856

Pennsylvania
Philadelphia
Jennifer Goldstein
(215) 731-0977

Pittsburgh
Amy Krut
(412) 885-2233

Valley Forge
Keith Miller
(215) 489-3705

Yardley
Brian Haugen
(609) 397-3366

South Carolina
Charleston
Debbie Martin
(803) 389-4921

Hilton Head Island
Maggie Metheney
(803) 686-6996

Texas
Austin
Tom Giebink
(512 447-0780
Jeff Hammett
(512) 450-0130

Dallas
Jamie Kastner
(817) 545-2459

Virginia
Alexandria
Greg Keim
(800) 252-3464

Annandale
Mark Freiden
(703) 941-8084

Burke
Richard Steidl
(703) 239-1611
Nicolas Perna
(703) 631-4118

Centreville
Nicholas Perna
(703) 631-4118

Fairfax
Krista Heubush
(703) 641-9773
Julie McKinstry
(703) 273-1069
Tricia Lewis
(703) 378-7601

Maryfield
Todd Karminski
(703) 385-1796

McLean
Peter Moog
(703) 790-4668

Oakton
Scott Roland
(703) 281-1254

Richmond
Ames Russell
(804) 354-9994

Vienna
Matt Titus
(703) 761-3040

Washington
Camas
Penny Wagoner
(206) 835-8485

Seattle
Dave Longmuir
(206) 725-6212

Wyoming
Laramie
Shawn Harris
(307) 721-2908

ORGANIZATIONS

Amateur Speedskating Union of the United States (ASU)
National Office
1033 Shady Lane
Glen Ellyn, IL 60136
(800) 634-4766
(708) 790-3230

Founded: 1927

The ASU is a non-profit organization run by volunteers whose goal is to develop speed skaters in the United States. The Union helps clubs by offering information, publishing a national magazine, and developing promotional material to be used on the local and national level. As a regulating body for competition in the United States, the ASU holds an annual conference to ensure the continued viability of the rules.

The ASU conducts summer training camps for skaters of all ages in various locations across the country. In winter months, Junior National and World Teams are selected to gain further experience in competition. The Junior National Team skates at the Olympic Festival every summer, which is to give young skaters a taste of the Olympic experience.

American Street Hockey Institute (ASHI)
P.O. Box 550
Winchendon Springs, MA 01477

To learn more about street hockey or beginning a street hockey league, send for the following booklet(s), available from ASHI:

• Official Open Area and Half Court Rules (including "How to Organize a Basic League") — $2
• ASHI Handbook and Official Rules — $4
• How to Organize a League — $2
• Referee Guidelines — Rink — $2
• Coaching Guidelines — Rink — $2
• Complete DEK HOCKEY Rink Information Package — $10

International In-Line Speedskating Association (IISA)
Lake Calhoun Executive Center
3033 Excelsior Blvd., Suite 300
Minneapolis, MN 55416
(800) FOR-IISA

Founded: July 1991

In-line skate manufacturers, athletes, and supporters formed IISA in July 1991. The group, an outgrowth of Rollerblade In-line Skating Association (RISA), was formed to develop a single, unified organization specifically for in-line skating.

Since its formation, the IISA has formed a twelve-person Steering Committee that defeated proposed skate bans in many American cities. The IISA also spearheaded a SKATESMART safety campaign in which manufacturers distributed millions of safety posters, fliers, and hang tags to retailers and consumers.

In October 1992, seven manufacturers became charter members of the IISA: Bauer®, CCM®, Kryptonics®, Rollerblade®, Roller Derby, Ultra Wheels™, and Variflex®. In December 1992, the seven charter members and in-line athletes formed a twelve-person Board of Directors, a five-person Executive Committee, and standing committees on Budget/Finance, Competition, Government Relations, Membership, Nominations, Public Relations, and Safety and Special Products. LaBeda Manufacturing, The Hyper Corporation, Get More Co., Ltd., Good-Men Associates Inc., and Asia Access, Inc., have also became Corporate Members of the IISA.

The objectives of the association are:
* To develop in-line safety and education programs.

* To protect and expand access for in-line skaters to streets, sidewalks, roads, highways, trails, and other public places.

* To work closely with the IISA Competition Committee (IISA/CC) to develop a first-rate sports program for in-line racers, hockey players, skiers, and freestyle athletes.

* To provide IISA members with excellent customer services.

(From the International In-Line Skating Association, Minnesota, 1991.)

If you have started a new club, have an upcoming in-line competitive event, or have information on roller hockey leagues, IISA would love to hear from you.

National In-Line Hockey Association (NIHA)
1221 Brickell Avenue
9th Floor
Miami, FL 33131
(800) 358-NIHA (members only)
(305) 358-8988 (head office)
(305) 374-4754 (members' fax)
(305) 358-8846 (administration fax)

Founded: January 1993

The NIHA is an amateur organization founded to govern the sport of in-line hockey. With the sponsorship of Rollerblade®, Inc. and the sanctioning of the IISA, the National In-Line Hockey Association is hierarchically organized from the bottom up. From team captains to local, state, and regional coordinators, the NIHA oversees the sport, providing organizational support and assistance.

Among the NIHA stated goals:
1. To attract as many member participants as possible.
2. To establish and periodically revise a standardized set of rules and regulations adhered to by all participants.

National Inline Speedskating Association
P.O. Box 3905
Costa Mesa, CA 92626
(714) 545-1800
(714) 741-6521 (Registration)

The National Inline Speedskating Association was launched to serve the growing number of in-line skaters and to promote their sport as a whole. Among its founding principles are: (1) it does not compete against other organizations and (2) it supports other organizations sharing its mission of serving the athlete, preserving and promoting the sport, and sponsoring in-line programs and competitive events.

Ontario Speed Skating Association
1220 Sheppard Avenue East
Willowdale, Ontario
Canada M2K 2X1
(416) 495-4043
Fax: (416) 495-4329

The Ontario Speed Skating Association was formed to act as a governing body for speed skating in Ontario. Presently, there are 1,000 active members, with an annual growth rate of between twenty and thirty percent.

Objectives of the group are:

1. To promote amateur speed skating.
2. To foster interest in blade skating including recreational, long distance, and marathon.
3. To develop skating facilities.
4. To promote the education of coaches and officials.

Outdoor Marathon Rollerskating Association (OMRA)
P.O. Box 181
Pine Lake, GA 30072
(404) 294-6351
Founded: 1986

OMRA sanctions long-distance (fifty kilometer and above) outdoor skating races, and awards points toward the annual North American Cup series. Some 1,000 names are included on the mailing list.

Outdoor Rollerskating Association of America (ORAA)
1855 Oak Street
San Francisco, CA 94117
(415) 752-8776
(415) 861-5214
Founded: March 1988

ORAA was founded when David Miles of San Francisco discovered that the industry lacked an organized, sensible structure. The organization was developed to launch his plan of ultimately dividing the entire country into independent regions. As conceived, teams within a given region compete. The team with the highest winning percentage would then compete against one of its neighboring regions. "The rest is academic," says Miles. Like the four divisions in baseball, each winning team would advance until there were just two left.

Ultimately, Miles will run for Executive Directorship of this organization. A skating organization of the skaters, elected by their fellow skaters, would guide the organization. Miles feels that any organization that can work with the community and show skating as a positive activity can achieve a mutual understanding through compromise. After all, he says, "It's better for young people to get involved in skating than in drugs, gangs, or crime." Miles was nominated by President Bush for the National Points of Light Award in 1990.

United States Amateur Confederation of Roller Skating (USAC/RS)
P.O. Box 6579
Lincoln, NE 68506
(402) 483-7551

Founded: 1937

USAC/RS was founded in 1937 as a part of the Roller Skating Rink Operators Association. Independently incorporated in 1973 and formally separated in 1987, USAC/RS is recognized as the official National Governing Body (NGB) for all competitive roller sports in the United States. Originally based in Detroit, Michigan, the Confederation moved to its present location in Lincoln, Nebraska in 1968.

Twenty-three thousand members and more than 1,600 skating clubs across the country compete in three skating disciplines: artistic, speed, and roller hockey. Athletes participate in a variety of contests, tournaments, and championships in a typical season, which runs from September through the following August.

Other USAC/RS duties include: maintaining and updating athlete information and records; providing training and educational opportunities for athletes and coaches; handling travel arrangements for domestic and international outings; fielding Team USA in each skating discipline; setting and enforcing competitive rules; determining competitive divisions; and working for the promotion and publicity of roller skating and its athletes both at home and abroad.

MUSEUM

The National Museum of Roller Skating
4730 South Street
Lincoln, NE 68506
(402) 483-7551

Founded: 1980

The National Museum of Roller Skating is a non-profit educational institution. Visitors can enjoy learning about the world of roller skating as sport, recreation, entertainment, and business. The museum collects skates, costumes, medals, trophies, photographs, posters, programs, and books concerning the world of roller skating.

In addition, the museum features exhaustive archival collections on the history of artistic skating, speed skating, and roller hockey. Visitors will also find a generous video library. The topics include: the United States Championships, rare Olympic and Pan American Games footage of athletes receiving their medals, as well as other roller skating events dating back to the 1940s.

OLYMPIC ORGANIZATIONS

United States International Olympic Committee
Olympic House
1750 East Boulder Street
Colorado Springs, CO 80909
(719) 632-5551
(719) 578-4529 (Public Relations)

International Olympic Committee
Chateau de Vidy
CH-1007 Lausanne
Switzerland
(41.21) 25 3271/3272

Atlanta Olympic Organizing Committee
Suite 3450, One Atlantic Center
1201 West Peachtree Street
Atlanta, GA 30309
(404) 874-1996

Games of the XXVIth Olympiad. Tentative Dates: July 20 to August 4, 1996.
USA Hockey
2997 Broadmoor Valley Road
Colorado Springs, CO 80906
(719) 576-4990

United States Field Hockey Association
1750 East Boulder Street
Colorado Springs, CO 80909
(719) 578-4567

Field Hockey Association of America
1750 East Boulder Street
Colorado Springs, CO 80909
(719) 578-4587

IN-LINE HOCKEY LEAGUES

Alabama

Birmingham
Birmingham Hockey League
(205) 933-1609

Huntsville
Serve & Volley League
(205) 880-3340

Hills Roller Hockey
5000 Whitesburg Drive
Huntsville, AL 35802
(205) 883-9917

Arizona

Phoenix
Skate World Hockey League
(602) 860-2844

Slap Shot
3632 E. Thomas Road
Phoenix, AZ 85018
(602) 956-1586

Scottsdale
Skate World Roller Hockey
11198 E. Laurel Lane
Scottsdale, AZ 85259
(602) 234-0312

California

Agoura
Tri Valley Hockey League
30772 Mainmont Drive
Agoura, CA 91301
(818) 706-8757

Anaheim
Anaheim Fun Center Roller
Hockey
2122 E. 20th Street
Santa Ana, CA 92701
(714) 835-3123

Chico
Cal State Hockey League
(805) 772-7851

Campus Bikes Roller Hockey
501 Main Street
Chico, CA 95928
(916) 345-2081

Claremont
City of Claremont Roller
Hockey
840 N. Indian Hill Blvd.
Claremont, CA 91711
(714) 399-5495

Fresno
Fresno Hockey League
(209) 625-4363

Fullerton
National Roller Hockey
League
1501 E. Chapman Avenue,
#331
Fullerton, CA 92631-4009
(714) 274-7545

Isla Vista
Skate World Hockey
(805) 685-0055

Lakewood
Kings Slapshot
5835 E. Carson Street
Lakewood, CA 90713
(310) 425-7431

Lompoc
Lompoc Roller Hockey
Village Skate Center
Vulcan Drive
Lompoc, CA 93436
(805) 733-3036

Los Angeles
Kings Slapshot
8808 S. Sepulveda Blvd.
Los Angeles, CA 90045
(310) 215-1084

Los Angeles Hockey League
(310) 838-6611

Morro Bay
Filippo's Roller Hockey
220 Atascadero Road
Morro Bay, CA 93442
(805) 772-7851

North Hollywood
Valley Roller Skating
(818) 980-0414

Norwalk
Norwalk Ice Arena
14100 S. Shoemaker
Norwalk, CA 90650
(310) 921-5391

Palmdale
Hockey Central
2111 E. Palmdale Blvd.
Palmdale, CA 93550
(805) 274-2424

Poway
North County Dek Hockey
14530 Espola Road
Poway, CA 92704
(619) 748-4260

Riverside
Riverside Hockey League
(714) 672-2944

Rolland Heights
California Street Hockey
Association
(818) 964-0590

San Diego
National Hockey Locker
9460 "F" Mica Mesa Blvd.
San Diego, CA 92126
(619) 578-4614

San Diego Hockey League
(619) 436-2901

San Francisco
San Francisco Hockey
League
(415) 446-3840

San Francisco/Oakland
Bay Area In-Line Hockey
2975 Van Ness, #22
San Francisco, CA 94123
(415) 904-8238

San Jose
Roxy's Roller Rink
397 Blossom Hill Road
San Jose, CA 95123
(408) 226-1156

San Juan Capistrano
City of San Juan Capistrano
Roller Hockey
31421 La Matanza
San Juan Capistrano, CA
  92675
(714) 493-5911

Santa Ana
Camelot Roller Hockey
2122 E. 20th Street
Santa Ana, CA 92701
(714) 835-7812

Kings Slapshot
3382 S. Bristol
Santa Ana, CA 92704
(714) 549-0290

Santa Ana Roller Hockey
2915 W. La Verne
Santa Ana, CA 92704
(714) 557-7501

Santa Barbara
Skater's Paradise
537 Skate Street
Santa Barbara, CA 93101
(805) 962-2526

Santa Clarita
Santa Clarita Hockey League
(805) 254-9740

Sherman Oaks
Kings Slapshot
13754 Ventura Blvd.
Sherman Oaks, CA 91423
(818) 784-4846

Venice
Venice Roller Works
7 Westminster
Venice, CA 90291
(310) 450-0669

Visalia
Central California Roller
Hockey
5149 Heritage
Visalia, CA 93277
(209) 625-4363

Whittier
Whittier Skateland
12520 E. Whittier Blvd.
Whittier, CA 90602
(310) 696-6779

Connecticut
Waterbury
Waterbury Dek Hockey
P.O. Box 3276
Waterbury, CT 06705
(203) 757-8381

Delaware
Newark
C & M Family Fun Spot
7 Eastwind Court
Newark, DE 19713
(302) 366-1664

New Castle Street Hockey
506 Four Season Parkway
Newark, DE 19702
(302) 731-7549

Florida
Fort Lauderdale
Fort Lauderdale Roller
Hockey
1900 E. Sunrise Blvd.
Fort Lauderdale, FL 33304
(305) 764-8800

Fort Lauderdale Hockey
League
(407) 985-3960

Miami
A Place for Wheels
West Kendall Roller Hockey
13001 N. Kendall
Miami, FL 33186
(305) 386-2453

American Roller Hockey
League
(305) 386-2453

River Forrest
Gunzo's
7706 W. Madison
River Forrest, FL 60305
(800) 776-4625

Georgia

Doraville
Roller Hockey League
6855 Ramundo Drive
Doraville, GA 30360
(800) 322-6334

Stone Mountain
Atlanta Street Hockey
5127 Leland Drive
Stone Mountain, GA 30083
(404) 498-1511

Illinois

Hoffman Estates
Poplar Creek Sports Centre
2350 Hassel Road
Hoffman Estates, IL 60195
(708) 884-0919

Massachusetts

Fitchburg
Fitchburg Street Hockey
27 Clark Street
Fitchburg, MA 01420
(508) 345-0265

Hingham
South Shore Sports Center
100 Recreation Park Drive
Hingham, MA 02043
(617) 740-1105

Hudson
Hudson Street Hockey
307 Cox Street
Hudson, MA 01749
(508) 562-3640

Lawrence
Lawrence Street Hockey
Lawrence Recreation Dept.
147 Haverhill Street
Lawrence, MA 01841
(508) 537-6711

Saugus
Hockey Town-Dek Hockey
953 Broadway, Route 1
Saugus, MA 01906
(617) 233-3666

Stoughton
Stoughton Recreation Center
57 French Street
Stoughton, MA 02072
(617) 341-4776

Michigan

Dearborn
Ford Woods Hockey League
(313) 582-4004

Eastpointe
Detroit Roller Hockey
Association
16850 Stricker
Eastpointe, MI 48021
(313) 775-7555

Mt. Clemens
Mt. Clemens Y.M.C.A. Floor
Hockey
10 W. River Road
Mt. Clemens, MI 48043
(313) 468-1411

Minnesota

Minneapolis
Dangl Roller Hockey
P.O. Box 6104
Minneapolis, MN 55406
(612) 491-2113

Twin Cities Hockey League
(612) 425-0311

St. Paul
Strauss Skate
1751 E. Hope Avenue
St. Paul, MN 55109
(612) 770-1344

Missouri

Florissant
Florissant Roller Hockey
10 Industrial
Florissant, MO 63031
(314) 839-0515

St. Louis
Ron's Roller World
120 E. Catalan
St. Louis, MO 63111
(314) 638-9002

Webster Ice Rink Hockey
League
(314) 727-2901

New Jersey

Bayonne
Bayonne Hockey League
(201) 858-1025

Linderwold
Tansboro Hockey
787 Emerson Avenue
Linderwold, NJ 08021
(609) 784-1336

Phillipsburgh
Easton Ball Hockey
290 Prospect Street
Phillipsburgh, NJ 08865-
1343
(908) 454-5040

Riverside
Riverfront Street Hockey
800 Carroll Street
Riverside, NJ 08075
(609) 764-7726

New York

Bellmore Long Island
Bellmore Merrick Roller
Hockey
104 Mitchell Street
Bellmore Long Island, NY
   11710
(516) 221-8477

Brooklyn
New York Hockey League
(718) 275-0970

East Stauket
Power Play Indoor Street
Hockey
80 Comsequoque Parsonage
Road
East Stauket, NY 11733
(516) 474-2260

Elmont
North Shore Dek Hockey
86 Barbara Street
Elmont, NY 11003
(516) 928-8901

Kew Gardens
Queens Roller Hockey
League
124-28 Queens Blvd.
Kew Gardens, NY 11415
(718) 275-0970

Latham
Randall's at the Knick
200 Oakwood Road
Latham, NY 12180
(518) 273-8305

Monroe
Upper New York Hockey
League
(914) 783-2575

Ridge
Mayer Dek Hockey
37 Woodlot Road
Ridge, NY 11961
(518) 588-7839

Ohio

Kettering
Hockey World
2900 Glengarry Drive
Kettering, OH 45420
(513) 294-2966

NE Canton
Canton Roller Hockey
2222 Cathy Drive
NE Canton, OH 44705
(216) 456-3806

Pennsylvania

Coraopolis
Western Area Y.M.C.A. Dek
Hockey
RD #1, Box 195
Coraopolis, PA 15108
(412) 787-3430

Finleyville
South Park Dek Hockey
P.O. Box 16
Finleyville, PA 15332
(412) 348-5276

Gibsonia
North Hills Dek Hockey
4457 Gibsonia Road, Route
910
Gibsonia, PA 15044
(412) 443-7825

Glenshaw
The Penalty Box
1302 Route 8
Glenshaw, PA 15116
(412) 487-5655

Lancaster
Lancaster Recreation —
Street Hockey
525 Fairview Avenue
Lancaster, PA 17603
(717) 392-2115

Middletown
Central Pennsylvania
Hockey League
1733 E. Harrisburg Pike
Middletown, PA 17057
(717) 944-7866

Oakdale
Dek Star North-Dek Hockey
Center
119 W. Steuben Street
Oakdale, PA 15071
(412) 695-2050

Pittsburgh
Dek Star North-Dek Hockey
Center
519 Mt. Nebo Road
Pittsburgh, PA 15237
(412) 366-4777

Penn Hills Dek Hockey
517 Twin Oak Drive
Pittsburgh, PA 15235
(412) 793-1966

Quebec, Canada

Beauport
Dek Hockey Quebec, Inc.
2475 Ave. St.-Viateur
Beauport, Quebec G1E 6E8
Canada
(418) 663-9661

Levia
Lauzon
200 Route Mgr. Bourget
Lewis, Quebec G6V 2I9
Canada
(418) 663-9661

Rhode Island

Cranston
Cranston Street Hockey
54 Potter Street
Cranston, RI 02910-3407
(401) 942-8088

Cumberland
New England Dek Hockey
Center
30 Old Diamond Hill Road
Cumberland, RI 02864
(401) 334-1081

South Carolina

Mt. Pleasant
Street and Roller Hockey
League
1460 Pine Island View
Mt. Pleasant, SC 29464
(803) 884-4517

Summerville
Summerville Hockey Club
102 Summer Road
Summerville, SC 29485
(803) 873-9406

Texas

Fort Worth
Rollerland West Hockey
League
(817) 735-4794

Richardson
Hotwheel's Richardson
816 S. Sherman Street
Richardson, TX 75081
(214) 231-0430

Spring
Champions Rollerworld
5504 Fellowship Lane
Spring, TX 77379
(713) 370-0750

Washington

Spokane
Spokane Hockey League
(509) 838-5159

Bibliography

Bay Area Inline Racers. Newsletter. Menlo Park, CA, 1992.

Beach Bladers of South Florida. Newsletter. Delray Beach, FL, 1992.

BladeTech Corporation. Promotional brochure. New Middletown, OH, 1992.

BNQ Accessories. Promotional material. Santa Monica, CA, 1992.

Brooslin, Michael W. *The First Fifty Years: American Roller Skates 1860-1910*. Lincoln, NE: National Museum of Roller Skating, 1983.

Brown, Chris H., M.D. "What's Up Doc?" *Skate News*, May/June 1992. Canstar Sports USA, Inc. Promotional brochure. Swanton, VT, 1992.

Chang, Gary. Letter to author, June 14, 1992.

Clifford, Mike. Letter to author, 1992.

Connecticut In-Line Skating Association. *Skeeler*, Vol. 1, No. 1, 1992.

Courtesy Sports. Promotional brochure. Los Altos, CA, 1992.

Directory. *Street Hockey Magazine*. Sept/Oct 1992, pp. 44-45.

Dow, Ted. "Taking Them on the Road." *InLine*, June/July 1992, p. 12.

Dowling, Jeff. Letter to author, June 16, 1992.

Etto AB. Promotional brochure and letter to the author. Stockholm, Sweden, 1992.

Evans, Harold, Brian Jackman, and Mark Ottaway. *We Learned to Ski*. New York: St. Martin's Press, 1974.

Feineman, Neil. *Wheel Excitement: The Official Rollerblade® Guide to In-Line Skating*. New York: Hearst Books, 1991.

First Team Sports, Inc. Press kit. Mound View, MN, 1992.

French, Diane, and Andrew Tilin. "A Pair of Skates in Every Home." *InLine*, August/September 1991, p. 7.

Gold, David. Skate City Supply Inc. Letter to the author, July 9, 1992.

Goldsun, Reverend Michael. Interview with author. San Francisco, CA, August 3, 1992.

Gross, David M. "Zipping Along in Asphalt Heaven: Rollerblade Streaks to Success." *Time*, August 13, 1990, p. 56.

"Guerrilla Marketing 101." *Working Woman*, December 1991, p. 23.

Hansen, Brian. Letter to author, July 1992.

"High Technology." *Speedskating Times*, March 1992, p. 37.

Howard, Thomas C. Letter to author, June 25, 1992.

Hyper Inline. Promotional brochure. 1992.

Ingles, Douglas. "Beginning In-line." *Speedskating Times*, June 1992, p. 8.

"Inline Goes Big Time." *Speedskating Times*, April 1992, p. 11.

In-line Skates: They Aren't Just for Kids." *Consumer Reports*, August 1991, p. 515.

Inline USA. Catalog. Morrow Bay, CA, 1992.

International In-Line Skating Association. Newsletter. August and May issues, 1992.

John Joseph Merlin: The Ingenious Mechanic. Kenwood: Greater London Council, 1985.

Joyner, Stephen C. *The Joy of Walking: More Than Just Exercise*. Crozet, VA: Betterway Publications, Inc., 1992.

Kaese, Dean. Conversations with author. February 1993.

Kretchmar, Laurie. "On the Rise." *Fortune*, August 12, 1991, p. 94.

Kron, Kari J. Letter to author, May 7, 1992.

Kryptonics, Inc. Promotional brochure. Boulder, CO, 1992.

Lee, Elizabeth. "The Fittest Thing on Two Wheels." *American Health: Fitness, Body and Mind*, March 1990, p. 38.

Levin, Susanna. "Go Speed Racer." *California Wheeling*, April 1992, pp. 55-58.

—— "All Training is Not Equal." *California Wheeling*, June 1992, pp. 54-60.

License to Skate In-line. VHS, 30 minutes. Distributed by Pantheon Home Video, Phoenix, AZ, 1991.

Lowden, Jon. Conversation with author. February 1993.

M & A Smith Corporation. Promotional material. Wormleysburg, PA, 1992.

McFadden, John. Letter to author, July 1992.

McNulty, Karen. "Roll with It." *Science World*, September 1991, pp. 18-20.

Mireault, Joe. Conversation with author. February 1993.

—— National In-Line Hockey Association: The Leading Edge. Miami: NIHA, 1993.

Merrow, Josh. "Training Wheels." *InLine*, February/March 1992, pp. 24-25.

Miles, David G., Jr. Interview with author. San Francisco, CA, August 4, 1992.

Mitrovic, Milan. Letter to author, July 1992.

Mogema Skates. Promotional brochure. Holland, 1992.

Naegele, Bob, III. Conversation with author. February 1993.

National Museum of Roller Skating. *Historical Roller Skating Overview*. No. 8, Lincoln, NE, 1983.

——. *Historical Roller Skating Overview*. No. 10, Lincoln, NE, 1984.

——. *Historical Roller Skating Overview*. No. 11, Lincoln, NE, 1984.

——. *Historical Roller Skating Overview*. No. 13, Lincoln, NE, 1985.

——. *Historical Roller Skating Overview*. No. 14, Lincoln, NE, 1985.

——. *Historical Roller Skating Overview*. No. 15, Lincoln, NE, 1985.

——. *Historical Roller Skating Overview*. Special Issue, Lincoln, NE, 1985.

New York Road Skaters Association. Newsletter. 1992.

NL MFG, Inc. Promotional brochure. 1992.

Ontario Speedskating Association. Facsimile to the author. Ontario, Canada, 1992.

Paragon Racing Products. Specifications sheet. Shakopee, MN, 1992.

Parcells, Charlie. "Pavement Distress." *InLine*, September 1991, pp. 34, 36.

Philpott, D. "A Skate of Change as New In-Lines Gain in Popularity." *Hockey Today*, 1990/1991, pp. 133-134.

Pritikin, Nathan. *The Pritikin Program for Diet and Exercise*. New York: Bantam Books, 1984.

Pyle, Glen. Letter to author, July 29, 1992.

Rappelfeld, Joel. *The Complete Blader*. New York; St. Martin's Press, 1992.

Riedell Shoes Inc. Promotional brochure. Red Wing, MN, 1992.

Rollerblade®. *Why Rollerblade*. Minneapolis, MN, 1992.

Rollerguard®. Press kit. Richmond Hill, Ontario, Canada, 1992.

"Rollermania." *City Sports*, July 1992, pp. 42, 45, 46.

"Runner's Knee." *City Sports*, July 1992, pp. 36, 37.

Ryan, Timothy. "Get Your Bearings." *InLine*, October/November 1991, p. 21.

Schafer, Lee. "It's Not a Fad." *Corporate Report Minnesota*, April 1992, pp. 31-38.

Shute, Nancy. "Blading with the Bad Girls." *Snow Country*, March/April 1992, pp. 66-70.

Skate Pro Sports. Promotional material. San Francisco, CA, 1992.

Sorenson, Barbara. Letter to author, July 15, 1992.

Starr, Cecie, and Ralph Taggart. *Biology: The Unity and Diversity of Life*. Belmont, CA: Wadsworth Publishing Company, 1989.

"Stopping on a Time." *Street Hockey Magazine*. Feb/March 1993, pp. 30-33.

Strauss, R.H. "In-line Skating: A New Path To Fitness." *Physician and Sports Medicine*, August 1990, pp. 36, 38.

Suhrstedt, Jerry. "Ask 'Mr. Techno.'" *InLine Info*.

Sure-Grip International. Promotional brochure. South Gate, CA, 1991.

Team Karim. Specification sheets. Berkeley, CA, 1992.

Therrien, Lois. "Rollerblade is Skating in Heavier Traffic." *Business Week*, June 24, 1991, pp. 114-115.

Traub, Morris. "Skating Backwards." *Roller Skating Through the Years: The Story of Roller Skates, Rinks, and Skaters*, edited by Morris Traub, pp. 3-17. New York: William-Frederick Press, 1944.

Turner, James. *History of Roller Skating*. Lincoln, NE: Roller Skating Rink Operators Association of America, 1975.

United States Amateur Confederation of Roller Skating. Facsimile to the author. Lincoln, NE, 1992.

Walter, Hal. "Endangered Species." *InLine*, December/January 1992, pp. 10-15.

Werardi, Dian. Phone interview with author. September 9, 1992.

Yak Research. Promotional material. Oakland, CA, 1992.

Zak, Andy. "Hit the Road Jack." *Speedskating Times*, April 1992, p. 22.

Zandstra Sports. Promotional brochure. Holland, 1991.

Zuver, Henry G., III. Letter to author, April 27, 1992.

Endnotes

● ●

1. James Turner, *History of Roller Skating* (Lincoln, NE: Roller Skating Rink Operators of America, 1975), p. 1.

2. Morris Traub, *Roller Skating Through the Years* (New York: William Frederick Press, 1944), pp. 4-5.

3. Ibid., p. 5.

4. Turner, p. 5.

5. Ibid., p. 4.

6. Traub, p. 9.

7. Ibid., p. 7.

8. Ibid., pp. 14-15.

9. Ibid.

10. Ibid.

11. Information provided by Dwain Hebda of USAC/RS.

12. Author's estimate.

13. Author's estimate.

14. Jon Lowden of *InLine* magazine.

15. Jon Lowden, interview with author. July 1992.

16. Author's calculation.

17. William A. Pullen, M.D., Santa Monica, CA.

18. Charlie Parcells, "Techno," *In-Line*, April 1992, p. 33.

19. Joel Rappelfeld, *The Complete Blader* (New York: St. Martin's Press, 1992), p. 11.

20. Jon Lowden, interview with author. July 1992.

21. Jon Lowden, "Skater Lady," *InLine*, April/May 1992.

22. Charlie Parcells, "Pavement in Distress," *InLine*, Aug/Sept 1992, pp. 55-58.

23. Ibid.

24. Jon Lowden, "Skater Lady," *InLine*, April/May 1992.

25. Ibid.

26. Joel Rappelfeld, *The Complete Blader* (New York: St. Martin's Press), p. 46.

27. Rappelfeld, pp. 46, 48.

28.   Ibid.

29.   Ibid., p. 51.

30.   Rappelfeld, pp. 72, 73.

31.   Ibid., pp. 79-80.

32.   Ibid.

Index